IMAGES
of America

CATSKILL HOTELS

Judy Jacobs, the daughter of one of the brothers who owned the Karmel Hotel in Loch Sheldrake, is pictured in front of the resort's Junior Building in 1942. She recalls, "This area was close to the main building and guests did not have to walk down a hill to the pool. In front of me there was a large apple tree [unseen], which provided shade. The area was a favorite with the hotel guests." Note her Shirley Temple curls.

Irwin Richman

ISBN 0-7385-1161-7

First published 2003
Reprinted 2004

Published by Arcadia Publishing,
Charleston SC, Chicago IL, Portsmouth NH, San Francisco CA

Printed in Great Britain

Library of Congress Catalog Card Number: 2002116103

For all general information, contact Arcadia Publishing:
Telephone 843-853-2070
Fax 843-853-0044
E-mail sales@arcadiapublishing.com
For customer service and orders:
Toll-free 1-888-313-2665

Visit us on the Internet at www.arcadiapublishing.com

The Sky Hotel in Woodbourne evolved from a boardinghouse, the Sky House, established early in the 20th century. According to this postcard, published in the 1960s, the resort was still operated by founders Archie and Lillian Schwartz, who ran it as "an informal family resort high in the hills of Sullivan County . . . with new accommodations [including] private baths."

CONTENTS

Acknowledgments

The Catskill Institute, founded in the 1990s by a group of academics and resort professionals, is America's premier repository for Catskill memorabilia and information. Its very rich Web site can be accessed at www.brown.edu/Research/Catskills_Institute. Like all of those who write about the history of the Catskills, I must thank the modern pioneers whose work provides the basis for many of our studies. These include, first and foremost, Manville B. Wakefield (1924–1975), the official Sullivan County historian, whose *To the Mountains by Rail* introduced me to Catskill historical sources. *The Catskill Mountain House,* by Roland Van Zandt (1918–1991), is an exemplar of the possibilities of the integration of resort and cultural history. The massive work *The Catskills from Wilderness to Woodstock,* by Alf Evers (born in 1905), is marvelously inclusive. It is my privilege to have known Manville and Alf. I wish I had known Roland.

My colleagues and the staff at Pennsylvania State University, Harrisburg, have always helped me. Patti Mills, our acting dean of graduate studies and research, and Dr. Simon Bronner, the acting head of the School of Humanities, have been very supportive of my writings. Simon's mother still summers in the Catskills; Patti's mother never did. Our very efficient reference librarians helped me check many facts. The staff of the Biomedical Photographic Office at our sister institution, the Milton S. Hershey Medical Center, did some vital photographic work. Linda Seaman has turned my chicken-scratch handwriting into legible typescript.

Phil Brown—the president of the Catskill Institute, a professor of sociology and environmental studies at Brown University, and a "mountain rat" who worked at Catskill hotels from age 13 until he entered graduate school—has been a mentor and a good friend.

My wife, Susan, a mathematician and of Pennsylvania German heritage, has adapted well to the Catskills. Our children, Alexander and Joshua, spent many summer days in the southern Catskills and also have very fond and continuing memories of the Mohonk Mountain House. Our daughter-in-law Kristin is the mother of our grandchildren, Benjamin David and Zoë Elizabeth Anne; all three need more Catskills in their young lives.

INTRODUCTION
1,115 HOTELS AND COUNTING

Generations of travelers and excursionists sailing up and down the lordly Hudson River saw it in the distance—a hulking, majestic Greek-porticoed white building, high on an escarpment beyond the town of Catskill. Standing until it was destroyed by the New York State Department of Conservation in 1964, the landmark was the Catskill Mountain House, the first great resort hotel in America. It was the flagship of an enterprise that eventually launched at least 1,114 other hotels. New York's Catskill Mountains once housed the greatest concentration of resorts that America had seen. Some were opulent, and others were quite modest. The early resorts catered to a Christian-only population, but beginning in the 1890s, vacation spots in the Fleischmann-Tannersville-Hunter region began to admit Jewish guests. Eventually, after more than a century of exclusion, the Catskill Mountain House itself became a Jewish resort, as did its chief rival, the largest hotel ever built in the Catskills, the 1,200-room Hotel Kaaterskill. Other smaller hotels remained exclusionary until the passage of civil rights legislation in the late 1960s—and some even beyond.

By the early 20th century, for many, the terms *Catskills* and *Jewish* were synonymous. This, in large part, is thanks to the development of the famed Borscht Belt in parts of Sullivan and Ulster Counties in the southern Catskills, or the Shawangunks. In the northern Catskills, the "real Catskills," German Jews broke down the religion barrier. In the Borscht Belt region, it was the Polish and Russian Jews. These latter were part of the 2.3 million Jews who immigrated to America between 1880 and 1924. They, too, wanted their place in the country—in the mountains, on the lakes, or along the swimmable rivers.

The early hotels of the northern Catskills were the products of steamboats that carried passengers up from New York City to the stagecoaches and wagons that would transport holiday travelers to the resorts. Trips were long, and sojourns were longer yet. Before the arrival of the railroad, it took three and a half hours of arduous travel to reach the Catskill Mountain House from the town of Catskill only 12 miles away—this after the long trip up the Hudson River. By 1892, the railroad had shortened the entire trip time from New York City to the hotel to under three and a half hours. Originally, visitors stayed for at least a month. Most lodged for the summer season. Guests would gossip and play cards, archery, and tennis. They would walk along carefully maintained mountain trails, take carriage rides, or row on the lake. Swimming later became popular. Mealtimes were festive, and guests customarily "dressed for dinner." There were church services on Sunday, and at the Catskill Mountain House, everyone had to get up before dawn (at least once) to watch the sun rise over the Hudson far below.

The grand hotels were expensive and catered to "a better sort." Numerous smaller establishments accommodated those of more limited means. The coming of the railroads democratized vacations and made the more affordable one-week stay possible. This trend toward shorter vacations, available to more people, was enhanced by the automobile.

Between the great resort area of the Hudson Valley and the foothills of Sullivan County are a series of remarkable mountaintop lakes, each in an extremely scenic location, high in the Shawangunks. Three of these lakes—Maratanza, Mohonk, and Minnewaska—were embellished with vast Victorian-era resort hotels. Two of these mountaintop retreats were owned by the Smiley brothers, twins Alfred and Albert, who built three hotels: the Lake Minnewaska Mountain House (later the Cliff House), the Wildmere, and the Mohonk Mountain House. While the hotels on Maratanza and Minnewaska are long gone, the Mohonk Mountain House, begun by Alfred Homans Smiley in 1879 and enlarged many times (lastly in 1910), is meticulously preserved. A National Historic Landmark, "the Mountain House is a turreted seven story architectural delight that stretches nearly an eighth of a mile along Lake Mohonk. The sight of this enchanting castle, with its sweeping lawns and vivid award-winning gardens never fails to thrill its visitors." While all of the hotel's mechanical systems and bathrooms are updated, "the Victorian character of the House has been preserved throughout, with beautifully carved woodwork, period furnishings, and cozy fireplaces found in many guest rooms, hallways, and parlors. Comfortable rockers line balconies and wide verandas," according to a recent (and honest) advertisement. The hotel, which was once restricted, now caters to a cosmopolitan clientele. In true Victorian style, afternoon tea is served, and until recently, no alcohol was served on premises. There is still no bar, but guests can order alcoholic beverages in the dining room. In another vestige of gentility, men are requested to wear jackets at dinner.

No such restraints exist at the last remaining resort hotels of the Borscht Belt to the south, where tee shirts and jeans are acceptable, if not preferred, dinner attire. Democracy and informality have triumphed here in the region once noted for its attention to elaborate dress and where black tie was once expected at dinner on Saturday nights at Grossinger's, one of the area's premier hotels.

The initial development of the resort industry of the southern Catskills is completely related to the railroad. The landlocked area was opened to tourism by the railroad eventually known as the New York, Ontario, and Western (O & W). Beginning in the 1870s, the railroad issued annual editions of *Summer Homes*, which promoted the scenic province. This newer resort area grew rapidly during what local historians consider the silver age. This was the Christian-only phase, and although Sullivan County had grand hotels such as Ye Lancashire Inn in Liberty (built in 1893–1894), it never really competed in grandeur with the region to the north. Rapidly it spawned myriad smaller hotels and boardinghouses, many of which catered to Irish and German immigrants who arrived by train for a week or two. Because of its high elevation and clean air, in addition to resorts, the Liberty region became the home to numerous tuberculosis sanatoriums. Vacationers were understandably wary of being near tuberculosis sufferers. Many hotels, accommodating vacationers' fears and prejudices, advertised, "No Hebrews or consumptives accepted."

Beginning in the 1890s, Jews from New York City started settling the locale, first as farmers drawn by the cheap land. Farmers soon became boardinghouse and hotel proprietors, and a newer industry was born. Hotels in the region can trace their development to two main sources, conveniently symbolized by the two most famous hotels in the Borscht Belt: Grossinger's and the Concord. The Grossinger family, like the Brickmans and Posners (Brickman's Hotel) and the Slutskys (Nevele Hotel), were farmers who, with their children, built great resorts. Others bought existing hotels. Real estate transactions changed the Sha-Wan-Ga Lodge and the White Roe Lodge instantly from "No Hebrews or consumptives allowed" houses to "Dietary Laws Observed" establishments. Most famously, Arthur Winarick set out to build the greatest hotel in Sullivan County. Using money earned from Jerris hair tonic and other toiletries, he built the extraordinary Concord. Where Grossinger's always prided itself on being *haimish* (homelike), the Concord was to become proudly sleek and modern.

The Borscht Belt became a separate-but-better-than-equal resort for New York's Jewish population. By the zenith of the golden age of the hotels, immediately following World War II, there were hundreds of hotels from which to choose. They ranged from *schlock* houses (dumps), little better than boardinghouses, to grand palatial establishments. It can be argued that the Catskill hotels made it possible for the masses to enjoy a luxury vacation. While rich businessmen and their families might spend a summer at Grossinger's or Brown's or the Laurels, their secretaries would save up for a week at the same places. Their accommodations might be more cramped (often two to a bed), but the facilities were the same—open to all. Hotels hired college boys to attract single girls, and the Catskills became one great marriage broker.

The hotels became known for their glitz and abundance; their guests, for their flamboyance. Hotels competed in offering ever more facilities. Guests demanded to know what was new each season, before making reservations. Swimming pools became filtered pools, followed by indoor pools. Indoor ice rinks also became a must. Food was everywhere. Meals were enormous and guests could order anything, or every item, on the menu. People were often proud of how many pounds they gained on vacation; this proved that they got their money's worth. Guests arrived with many suitcases, and women were expected to change clothes at least three times a day and never to wear the same dress twice in the dining room. By the mid-1950s, even before air conditioning became mandatory, every woman needed her mink stole for Saturday night, as well as a mink-trimmed cashmere sweater for less formal occasions. Entertainment ranged from the home grown to the biggest stars in the business, many of whom, such as Danny Kay and Sid Caesar, had developed in the Catskills. These were heady years, but they cranked down. What changed? Society did. Murray Posner, a co-owner of Brickman's in South Fallsburg, noted, "I used to have to compete with the hotel down the road. Now, I have to compete with the world." It was an uneven battle, and while most of the hotels died, the Catskill tradition of lavish hospitality lives on. It has merely traded venues.

It is no accident that the people who created or reinvented our most popular contemporary resort destinations had the Catskills in their past. Ben Novak, who grew up as the son of the owners of the Laurels Country Club in Monticello, would build Miami Beach's incredible Foutainbleu Hotel, which was the high point in the development of Miami Beach's lavish hotel life. However, many Catskill hotel owners also had hotels in Miami Beach, some as early as the 1920s. The Weiners of the White Roe Inn owned the Plymouth and the Adams hotels. The Levinsons built the Algiers, and the Grossingers bought the Pancoast, a restricted hotel whose clientele they changed. Bunny Grossinger tells the story of a longtime Christian guest of the Pancoast calling for his regular winter reservations. When told that management had changed and dietary laws were now observed, he replied innocently, "Good, I can use a diet." Steve Wynn, who has developed several of Las Vegas' most elaborate resorts, including the Bellagio, spent his summers at Grossinger's.

Even at its most Jewish time, the Catskills had hotels catering to other ethnic groups. Peg Leg Bates Hotel, opened by the famed entertainer, catered to African Americans. The Villa Roma in Calicoon still flourishes and attracts an Italian American crowd. While only two large old-style Jewish resorts survive in the Catskills today—Kutsher's Country Club and the Raleigh—the vital essence of the Catskills lives on. The spirit of over-the-top food and entertainment pioneered in the Catskills has simply changed location. Many of today's most popular cruise ships are nothing more than reconfigured Catskill-style resorts that float. The Catskill Institute, which maintains a list of mostly past and fewer present Catskill hotels, now counts 1,115 hotels. More names are always being added. More cruise ships are always being added, but their numbers will never match those of their inspiration. It is no accident that the principle owners of Carnival Cruise Lines are very familiar with the Catskills of yesterday. Let the good times sail.

Honeymooners Alexander and Bertha Richman are shown at the Woodbourne Sky House (see page 4) in August 1931. He was 24 and she was 15. Both spent at least part of every summer of their married life in the Catskills. She still does. In the 1920s and 1930s, the Catskills were the favored honeymoon destination for many of New York's Jewish couples.

One

The Classic Catskills

The Catskill Mountain House, the Catskills' first great hotel, was operating by 1824, and its site high above the Hudson River quickly became famous. Like everything popular in pre–Civil War America, the resort was illustrated in a lithograph, *Scenery of the Catskills*, published by famed New York printmakers Currier and Ives.

Poet William Cullen Bryant (1794–1878) was America's premier bard of nature and scenery. He was also the friend and patron of many artists, some of whose work he featured in the several editions of *Picturesque America* he published. The publication combined poetry and illustrations of American landscapes. Harry Fenn's *The Mountain House* was in the 1874 edition.

Harry Fenn's *The Mountain House* was clearly the source for this souvenir painting of the hotel painted on an artist's palette *c.* 1880. In addition to souvenir makers, many important artists painted the Mountain House, including Thomas Cole (1801–1848), Francis Jasper Cropsey (1823–1900), and Sanford Robinson Gifford (1823–1880).

Sailboats shared the Hudson with steamboats bringing clients for the Catskill Mountain House. Most passengers for the expensive, exclusive resort disembarked at the "Long Wharf" near the town of Catskill, as recorded in 1847 by local resident and artist Thomas Cole, whose nearby house, Cedar Lawn, is now a museum.

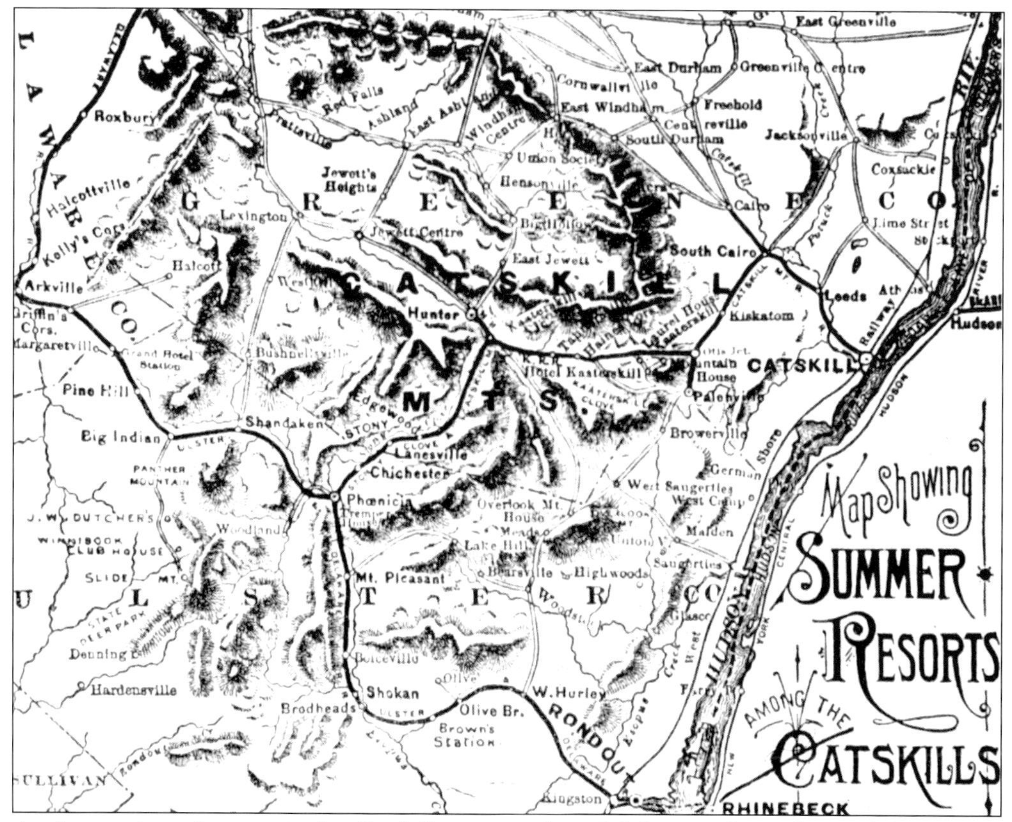

As the number of resorts in the Catskills increased, so did the populous who used the river as their vacation highway. A steamship company published this map in 1894, which also shows railroad lines.

The Catskill Mountain House, scenery painters, and photographers at work are all illustrated in Thomas Nast's *Sketches among the Catskill Mountains*, published in 1866. Nast (1840–1902) is best known as the artist who created our famed image of Uncle Sam. Note especially the vignette to the left of the grand hotel, which shows people on the magnificent portico of the Mountain House.

Before the coming of the railroad, it took about three and a half hours of bumpy stagecoach travel to cover the 12 miles from the village of Catskill on the banks of the Hudson to the Catskill Mountain House. By 1892, the railway from New York covered the entire 125-mile trip in the same amount of time. An Otis Elevated Railroad car carried travelers right up to the hotel. Day-trippers came in droves to enjoy the fabulous view, as in this *c.* 1900 stereopticon view. While still elegant, the Mountain House was clearly becoming less exclusive.

1823. 83d Season. 1905.

CATSKILL MOUNTAIN HOUSE,

CHAS. AND GEO. H. BEACH.
Managers.

CATSKILL N. Y.

Elevation 2,250 feet. Open June 26th.

The Only Hotel that Commands the Famous View of the Hudson River Valley.

THE MOUNTAIN HOUSE PARK

At the terminus of mountain branch of the Ulster & Delaware R. R. Has a valley frontage of over three miles in extent and consists of 2,780 acres of magnificent forest and farm lands, traversed in all directions by many miles of wood trails and carriage roads leading to points of interest.

THE GRANDEST VIEWS OF THE REGION

Are obtained from the Crest, Newman's Ledge, Bear's Den, Prospect Rock on North Mountain; and Eagle Rock and Palenville Overlook on South Mountain, which are included in the mountain house property.

NORTH AND SOUTH LAKES

Are also included within its boundaries. The atmosphere is delightfully pure.

ABSOLUTELY FREE FROM MALARIA.

The temperature is always 15 to 20 degrees lower than at Catskill village, New York City or Philadelphia.

A POWERFUL SEARCHLIGHT,

On the east front, will be operated from 9 to 11 P. M., reflecting its light over twelve thousand square miles of the Hudson River Valley. The hotel is lighted throughout by electric lights. Call and return call bells. Long distance telephone and telegraph office in the hotel. Sanitary plumbing.

THE WATER SUPPLY IS ABUNDANT.

The spring is over two miles distant, far up toward the crest of North Mountain, with nothing above or around, but a spruce and hemlock forest, and, as the land is owned by the Hotel Company, contamination is impossible.

THE OUT DOOR AMUSEMENTS.

The life in this invigorating air makes out door amusements especially sought for and enjoyed. The boat livery privilege has been granted to Messrs. Byles & Hoff, of Bayonne, New Jersey, who furnish canoes, out-riggers and row boats of the most approved pattern.

ACCESSIBLE BY FOLLOWING ROUTES:

Pennsylvania Railroad from Philadelphia, Washington and intermediate stations makes connections, and solid trains are run over the West Shore and Ulster & Delaware Railroads to Kaaterskill Station, located within the boundaries of the Catskill Mountain House Park, and only ¾ of a mile drive over a smooth, level road to the hotel.

VIA RHINEBECK, RONDOUT AND KINGSTON.

New York Central & Hudson River Railroad to Rhinebeck; Hudson River Day Line to Kingston Point; Rondout Night Line to Rondout; West Shore Railroad to Kingston; Ulster & Delaware Railroad to Kaaterskill Station; ¾ of a mile to the hotel. Stages meet all trains. Purchase tickets and check baggage to Kaaterskill Station.

RATES:

Daily, $3.00 and $4.00. Weekly, $17.50, $21.00 and $25.00. Special weekly rates for guests arriving before July 4th, for three weeks or the season. For day visitors, Table d' Hote Dinner, $1.00.

Still under the ownership of the founding Beach family in 1905, the Catskill Mountain House touted its attributes in an advertisement in *Catskill Mountain Resorts*, a promotional pamphlet distributed by the Ulster and Delaware Railroads, whose "Kaaterskill Station [was] located within the boundaries of the Catskill Mountain House Park." Americans today tend to think of malaria as a tropical disease, but until after World War I, it was common in much of the United States. Hence, the Catskill Mountain House proudly proclaimed itself "Absolutely Free from Malaria." Why? Because it is much colder than New York City and Philadelphia are.

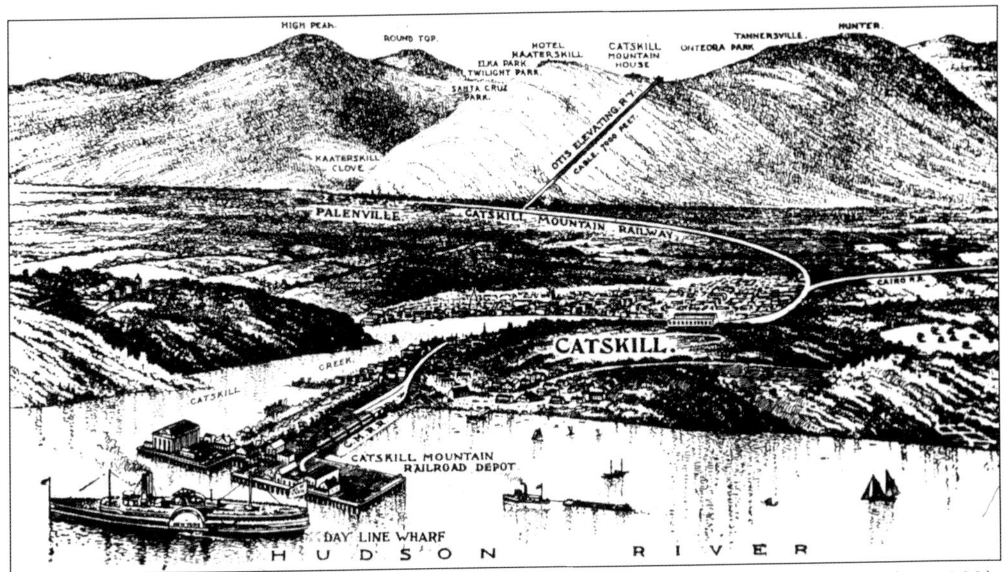

An engraving in a popular travel book, *Van Loan's Catskill Mountain Guide* (published in 1909), shows the 20th-century transportation system that led to the Catskills. High on the mountaintops were the Catskill Mountain House and its chief rival, Hotel Kaaterskill, as well as several private parks, including Onteora and Elka.

After World War I, the Catskill Mountain House lost its social cachet. No longer a fashionable site, the hotel was leased in the 1930s to Jacob Eli and David Andron, who changed its name and ran it as a kosher hotel. Because of wartime difficulties, the Androns ended their operation in 1942, and the hotel fell into ruin. Then owned by the state, the hotel was burned to the ground in 1962 by the New York State Department of Conservation.

The Laurel House was situated atop picturesque Kaaterskill Falls. Originally a small farm-hotel, it was enlarged after the Civil War and again between 1881 and 1884. *View from Prospect Rock: Kaaterskill Falls* appeared in A.E.P. Searing's 1884 *The Land of Rip Van Winkle*. The Laurel House was the longest-lived great hotel in the Catskills, surviving into the 1960s, when it was purchased by the New York State Department of Conservation.

In the 1880s, with its major additions in place, the Laurel House was the very picture of a grand Victorian resort where the fashionably dressed vacationers promenaded on well-landscaped grounds. The original hotel is now to the left of the grand portico (as seen from this perspective). The postcard view below, devoid of people but with more and larger trees, was sent in August 1906 to Nellie Gallagher in Lebanon, Pennsylvania.

Hotel visitors often explored the usually manicured wonders of nature on the grounds of their resorts and on those of neighboring resorts. Waterfalls were especially fascinating. After the Civil War, artist Winslow Homer (1836–1910), who had portrayed the horrors of wartime for *Harper's Weekly*, turned to report on the pleasures of vacations for the same magazine. His *Under the Falls: Catskill Mountains* appeared on September 14, 1872. Homer shows two elegant

young ladies, hiking staffs in hand, probably on the grounds of the Catskill Mountain House, observing the falls from a comfortable vantage point. A more adventurous couple is seen in the distance. Homer's views of resorts also included visits to the White Mountains and the New Jersey shore.

The 1,200-room Hotel Kaaterskill was built to provide direct competition to the Catskill Mountain Hotel. The spelling *Kaaterskill* was not old Dutch but rather an adaptation created by Emily Harding, whose husband, George W. Harding, built the grand hotel in 1881. Alas, this behemoth of a resort was short lived. When the ethnic composition of Catskill vacationers changed, the hotel was sold to Harry Tannenbaum, who converted it to a kosher establishment. In September 1924, it burned in a spectacular fire, which was seen all the way to Massachusetts. The illustration above is from *The Land of Rip Van Winkle*.

Squirrel Inn at Haines Falls was typical of the many refined smaller resorts that dotted the Catskills. Tudor in style, the hotel exuded an air of respectability. Mailed to Carrie Over of Allenhurst, New Jersey, this postcard bore a simple message: "Greetings from Your Pastor."

Sunset Park was one of several private enclaves of summer homes sprinkled through the Catskills. Most of these "parks" had an inn catering to "their kind of people." In other words, neither Catholics nor Jews needed to apply. Aunt Esther, writing to "Ella, Charles & Kiddies" in Windbar, New York, of her vacation, wrote on this card, "I have been too busy causing [me to be] all tired out."

Stamford in the Catskills was popularized by the legend of Utsayantha, a Native American girl who loved a white man and, when the love was thwarted by her father, plunged to her death in what has come to be called Lake Utsayantha. One of the most prominent promoters of the legend, which for a while was almost as popular as the Rip Van Winkle tale, was Dr. S.E. Churchill, the founder of the picturesque Churchill Hall Hotel (above). Other elegant hotels like the Rexmere followed, and Stamford developed as a major Christian-only resort community.

The automobile changed the Catskills, making the mountains and many of its deeper recesses easily accessible to everyone. While this ease of travel hurt the exclusiveness of the grand hotels, it helped many small resorts thrive. A Model T Ford is on the dirt road in front of Spring Brook Cottage in Big Indian on a postcard mailed in 1913. A streamlined 1930s automobile stands in front of the Shady Grove Hotel in Haines Falls. Proud as the hotel owners were of the automobiles, these cards emphasized the serenity of rural life, which is what the hotels were selling (or renting).

Many resorts preferred to project a rural image long after they had left their farming days behind. This was certainly the case with Shepard Farm in Greenville, which became a small, full-scale resort hotel. A 1930s vista of the exterior shows a farmhouse that grew in many directions. The 1960s view of the dining room displays no rural sensibilities at all; rather, with its cut-glass chandelier and wall sconces, it could be a hotel anywhere in America. As the Catskill resorts yielded to change, they often lost their distinctive flavor.

Two

CASTLES ON THE MOUNTAINTOP

The grand Queen Anne Revival hotel called the Mount Meenahga stood on the shore of Lake Maratanza, high on a mountainside above Ellenville. Never as renowned as its more northerly neighbors on Lakes Mohonk and Minnewaska, the Meenahga eventually burned. Acidic Lake Maratanza, with crystal-clear soft water and devoid of aquatic life, is now Ellenville's reservoir.

Lake Minnewaska, a glacial lake 1,650 feet above sea level, was developed by Albert Keith Smiley, whose twin brother built the nearby Mohonk Mountain House. The Lake Minnewaska Mountain House (above, right) was built in 1879 and enlarged in 1888. Its name was changed to the Cliff House in 1887. The resort estate covered 9,000 acres. Business was so good for Albert Smiley that he built a second hotel, the Wildmere, in 1888, which was expanded to its final size in 1910. It is seen above in an aerial view and below *c*. 1910.

The Cliff House was majestically poised above Lake Minnewaska and operated as a hotel into the second half of the 20th century, as attested to by the shorts-clad young golfers on the putting green. Both Victorian hotels—the Cliff House and its sister resort, the Wildmere—eventually burned. After much bitter squabbling, the state acquired the peerless hotel estate for a park in the late 1980s. The site is often used in television commercials urging tourists to visit scenic New York.

A dramatic feature at the Lake Minnewaska resorts and the Lake Mohonk Mountain House was the rustic gazebos placed along meticulously maintained paths and carefully sited to allow for viewing specific scenic delights. The gazebo shown was located on the "Under Cliff Trail" below the Cliff House. At Lake Mohonk, the gazebos are still maintained. Because of their exposed locations, they are rebuilt periodically for safety.

To increase revenue after the mid-20th century, the resorts on Lakes Minnewaska and Mohonk remained open year-round instead of their traditional May–October season. This postcard, mailed in the late 1960s, suggests that the hotel was on hard times. On September 22, Elise writes, "They ran out of summer cards," but "the meals [are] super." While the winter season was not a savior for the Cliff House (shown here), it has proved successful for Lake Mohonk, which today has completed an extraordinary outdoor ice-skating pavilion.

On July 4, 1859, John F. Stokes opened the first public house, Stokes Tavern, on Lake Mohonk. The scenic spot was recorded in a hand-colored lithograph produced by Currier and Ives. In 1869, Albert Smiley, a Philadelphia Quaker, bought the original 300-acre site for $28,000. In 1870, the former tavern was enlarged to accommodate 40 guests, and its name was changed to the Mohonk Mountain House. No liquor was served. The hotel is still owned by the Smiley family.

The Mountain House, a National Historic Landmark, was completed in 1910 and is an eighth of a mile long. The principal architects were Napoleon LeBrun (1821–1901), a Philadelphian who built the frame section to the left, and James E. Ware (1846–1918), a New York City resident who designed the towered stone section. The Albert K. Smiley Memorial Tower stands on the Mohonk estate's highest point.

The Albert K. Smiley Memorial Tower was the third tower built on Skytop (originally called Paltz Point). It was constructed to memorialize the Mountain House founder after his death in 1912. Profits from the hotel had enabled him to be very philanthropic, and he was active in movements to promote world peace. He was even nominated for the 1913 Nobel Peace Prize by the U.S. secretary of state, Elihu Root. From Skytop, visitors look out on the Wallkill and Rondout Valleys and can presumably see six states on a clear day.

In 1981, nine-year-old Alexander Richman and his seven-year-old brother, Joshua, pose on the Skytop tower. The hotel is far below. The Catskill Mountains are seen in the distance. Skytop can be reached by a winding footpath or a carriage road via a horse-drawn vehicle.

Extending over the lake is a grand two-story rustic pavilion housing deep porches lined with rockers, a favorite spot for guests to gather. On the lower level, guests are encouraged to feed the huge trout that congregate under the porch. At 4:00 p.m., tea is served in the adjoining Lake Side Lounge. In fair weather, many guests take their tea on the porch. In July 2002, Alexander Richman and Damon Merkle sit on one of the massive iron beams that support the pavilion. Bertha Levinstein sits on a rocker.

The massive main dining room at the Mohonk Mountain House is a symphony of polished wood. It retains its original lighting fixtures and, in summer, is cooled only by ceiling fans. Male guests are still requested to wear jackets at dinner, and most do.

In the 1950s, many people dressed more formally than they do today. While the 18-hole putting green near the hotel's east entrance looks much the same today, the guests' costume is often very different.

The Mohonk Mountain House promotes its historic past. Its brochures and menus are often illustrated with engravings, some of which were done by Elias J. Whitney (born in 1827). The original copper engraving plates for these illustrations were found in 1976 in the basement of the Picnic Lodge by Jim Clark, the curator of the Mohonk Barn Museum. They were in a box dated 1911 and marked "obsolete engraving plates—save for possible historic interest." Note that early gazebos were often thatched. Often rebuilt, this gazebo was a longtime favorite of the author's mother.

Mohonk
Mountain House

Rates and Policies
APRIL 2002 – MARCH 2003

All rates are per room, per night and include three meals daily plus Afternoon Tea and Cookies.

Complimentary recreational activities: Children's Programs (as scheduled), Boating, Tennis, Midweek Golf. Winter season: Ice Skating; Cross-Country Skiing and Snowshoeing (weather permitting). Additional charges for Horseback Riding, Carriage Rides, and Weekend Golf.

Daily Rates

Rates vary according to: view (garden, lake, or mountain); size; and décor

ROOM TYPES	SINGLE OCCUPANCY	DOUBLE OCCUPANCY
Traditional Style	$200-415	$335-515
Victorian Style *(with balcony and fireplace)*	$320-415	$420-515
Suites/Junior Suites	$420-520	$520-620
Tower Rooms	$540-570	$640-670

No charge for children under age 4.

Additional child (ages 4-12): $75.00

Adult (over age 12): $125.00

Most weekends require a two night minimum stay. Minimums for holiday weekends may vary. Please inquire about our theme programs and midweek special value rates.

For reservations that require meeting or function space, please call our Sales Office at (845) 256-2045.

Rates are subject to applicable state and local taxes. In lieu of all gratuities, a 15% service charge is added to your daily room rate. A 15% service charge will be added to beverage checks, room service, and massage. Rates are subject to change without notice.

For Reservations

Please call (800) 772-6646, or your Travel Agent
Fax: (845) 256-2100

The Mountain House at Lake Mohonk is the last surviving great hotel of the Catskills. While its future seems secure and the hotel is determined to preserve its authentic ambiance, it is obviously a very expensive operation to maintain. Additionally, it has quietly added new facilities and improved the food, which is now prepared by the award-winning Mohonk Culinary Team. The hotel looks quaint, but its prices are very modern. Compare these prices with those charged by the Catskill Mountain House in 1905 (see page 16).

Three

The Silver Age

This band played for summertime dances at the outdoor dance pavilion at Kraack's Hotel in Lake Huntington *c.* 1905. Waiter Will Kraack holds mugs of beer. Hotel owner Charles Kraack sits next to cello player George Merkensschlager. Jacob Keim was the first fiddler and caller, and rounding out the trio was Mike Busch.

Summer Homes was published by the New York, Ontario, and Western and its predecessor since 1878 to promote the region's resorts and boost the railroad's passenger load. Cover art was very sentimental, emphasizing an idyllic vacation or the region's bucolic nature. On the cover of this 1892 issue, a lovely lady sits beneath a parasol with a lake in the background. Note the hotel on the shore.

SULLIVAN COUNTY BUSINESS DIRECTORY. 297

Exchange Hotel,

MONTICELLO, N. Y.

LE GRAND MORRIS, PROPRIETOR.

Having purchased this old and well known Hotel and refitted and furnished it throughout, I am now prepared to furnish first class accommodations to transient or permanent guests, on reasonable terms.

The Tables will at all times be furnished with the delicacies of the season, and the Bar will be supplied with

Choice Wines, Liquors and Cigars.

Free "Bus" to and from all Trains. All Stages start from this Hotel.

LeGrand Morris.

O'NEILL'S LIVERY ATTACHED.

EXCHANGE HOTEL

Livery Stable!

J. D. O'NEILL & SON, PROPRIETORS.

MONTICELLO, N. Y.

Trusty Horses, the best of Carriages and Careful Drivers, at the service of the public.

Horses and Carriages for Parties and Excursions, or for Funerals.

We also run a Daily Line of Stages to connect with Trains on the Midland Railroad at Fallsburgh.

Monticello's Exchange Hotel was popular with business travelers, locals, and vacationers. Note that their stable could provide "Horses and Carriages for Parties and Excursions or for Funerals." A year after this advertisement appeared in the 1873 *Sullivan County Gazetteer and Business Directory*, a fire destroyed the whole complex, as well as "George Hindley's saloon, Kent's Barber Shop, The Republican Walchman printing plant, Billing's Floor and Feed Store, and Curley's Hotel." Owner Le Grand Morris had been very proud of his recently "refitted and furnished . . . old and well known hotel."

The coming of the Monticello and Fallsburg Turnpike in 1889 opened much resort land for development, and three years later, the Monticello and Fallsburg Tally-Ho Stage Line was founded. Here, the well-loaded stage prepares to depart from the Russell House in South Fallsburg on the trip to Sullivan County's seat, Monticello. Stages and other horse-drawn vehicles were in common usage into the 1920s.

The Mansion House, Monticello, N.Y.
Sweet Bros., Publishers.
MADE IN GERMANY

The original Mansion House was built in 1810, just a year after Sullivan County was organized. In subsequent years, it was greatly enlarged. In 1909, its name was changed to the Monticello Inn. Because of its clientele, it soon became known as the "actor's hotel." Very much altered, it still stands on Broadway in Monticello.

The architecture of the Pleasant View House clearly shows how a hotel could grow from a farmhouse. This card was mailed in 1921 to Lucile M. Alzamora, whose friend Pearl relates, "I do a great deal of crocheting and have little time for anything else. . . . I often wish I had a typewriter at my disposal. I'd write to everyone in Brooklyn."

The Park View House is the very model of a rambling yet modest Queen Anne Revival hotel on one of Liberty's side streets. Since it was located in town in Liberty, it quite possibly was open year-round, renting to consumptives in the winter.

With 300 rooms, the Hotel Wawonda was the largest resort built in Sullivan County during the silver age. Constructed in 1891–1892, it was soon reported to be "patronized by a very wealthy class of people coming from New York City, Philadelphia, and Washington." Business fell away, and after passing through several owners, the hotel burned in 1914.

Ye Lancashire Inn, built in 1893–1894, was open all year round, but it took no consumptives. A deluxe establishment, it boasted of "Steam and Hot Water Heat, Electric Lights [and] Modern Improvements." Interestingly, many wealthy Cubans had vacationed at the hotel, which (like the Wawonda) fell out of fashion. When it burned in 1920, it was being used as a hospital for World War I veterans.

Originally called Robertsonville, the town was renamed White Sulphur Springs by promoters who hoped that the local "odorous water" would turn the region into a spa like White Sulphur Springs in West Virginia. The White Sulphur Springs House, built in 1889, was to be the equivalent of West Virginia's Greenbrier Hotel. Originally very successful, the veranda-trimmed hotel lost its elite popularity after World War I, although it survived for many more years as a Jewish resort.

The Dew Drop Inn in Wurtsboro is one of many resorts nationally that adopted cute names in the 1920s. A handsome Colonial Revival building, it was in business well into the 20th century. Wurtsboro, a canal-era town, is in a valley, lower in altitude than most Catskill resort communities.

Lake Huntington had many hotels. Both Kraack's Hotel (see page 37) and the Sagamore had German proprietors and probably catered to an immigrant German clientele. The Sagamore (above) was probably named in emulation of the famous Sagamore Hotel on Lake George. The Viola House (below) is more modest in its name and looks like the overgrown farmhouse that it was.

White Lake is the largest lake in Sullivan County, but it was hard to reach before the Liberty and White Lake Turnpike was opened in 1886. The building of the turnpike set off a burst of hotel building around the white-sand-bottomed lake. It enabled guests to reach the area from Liberty via stagecoach. The Laurel House (above) faced the lake from a high rise. The Fulton House (below) was extensively remodeled in the 1920s, when its name was changed to the New Empire, and it became a kosher resort.

Saturday afternoon was a popular time for boating parties on White Lake, which was bordered by hotels when this 1909 view was taken. The towered Kenmore Hotel is seen on the far shore. It had a commanding view of the lake and what Manville B. Wakefield called "seemingly endless porches and balconies." It burned in 1947.

You will not find North White Lake on any modern map. Always a quieter community than nearby White Lake, it changed its name to Kauneonga Lake in the 1920s. The West Shore Hotel was a typical 1890s resort in the region. Notice its mansard roof, so popular on late-Victorian hotels.

Tennanah Lake, near Roscoe, is in western Sullivan County. Its oldest resort was the Lake Wood Farm, which burned in 1897 and was replaced with the Sunset Lodge, which burned in 1932. Longer lasting was the Tennanah Lake House, built by A. Peter Wolff early in the century. It was first advertised in the *Summer Homes* of 1907, when it accommodated 80 guests, and was enlarged substantially over the years. Many of its guests were German American.

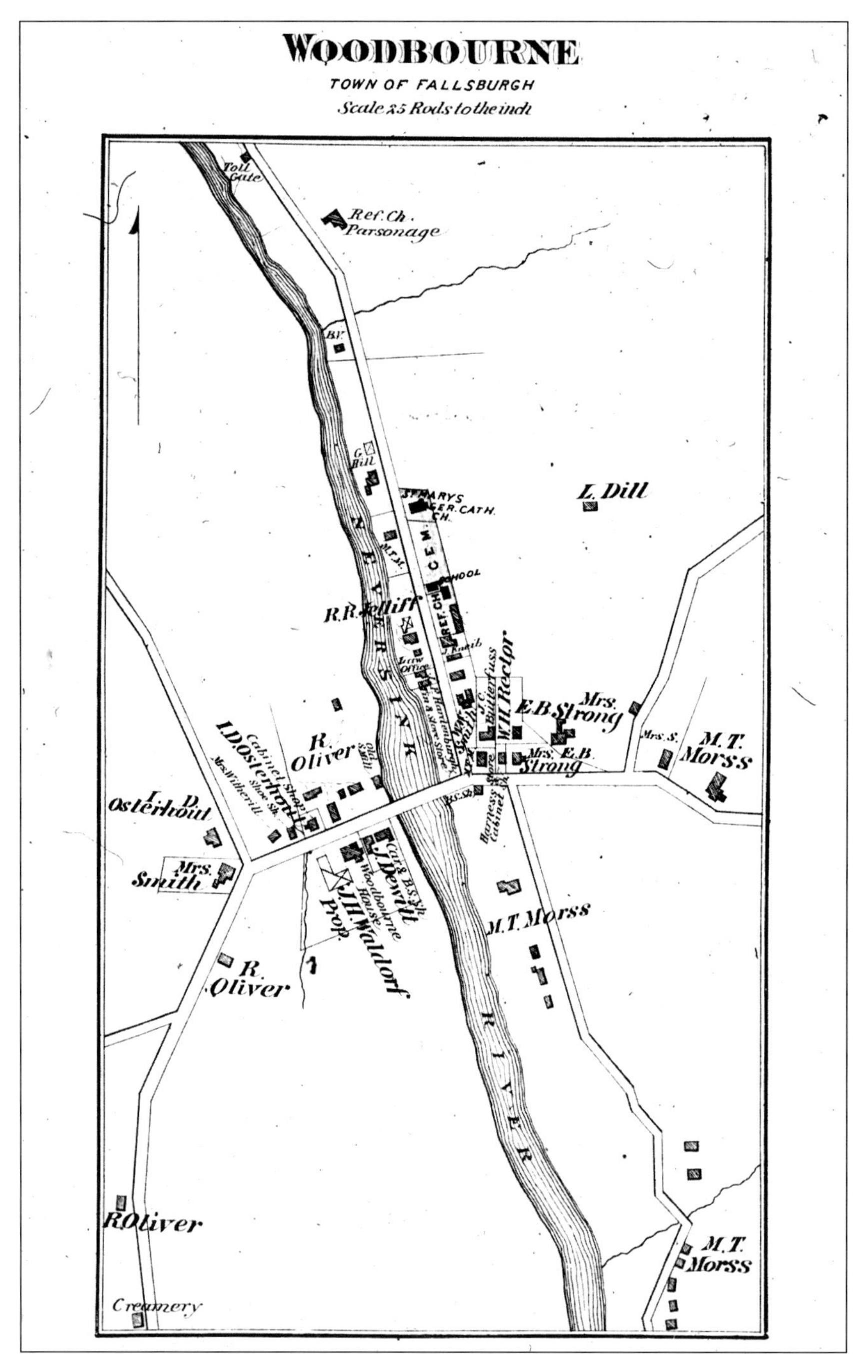

Woodbourne was a typical Sullivan County town in the late 19th century, before the hotel age hit. The town straddling the Neversink River had only one resort—the Woodbourne Hotel. In the 1906 edition of *Summer Homes* (a few years after road improvements and a new iron bridge across the river), there were 26 places. By 1903, the *Liberty Register* noted an ethnic shift in the community. "Hebrews have turned their attention toward Woodbourne and are buying up the purchasable farms in that section. During the past few days, they have bought Gus Hasbrouck's farm, one of the best there is for $6200. Wright Holmes farm for $1700."

232 *SULLIVAN COUNTY BUSINESS DIRECTORY.*

WOODBOURNE HOUSE!

John H. Waldorf,

PROPRIETOR,

Woodbourne, Sullivan County, N. Y.

This House has been refitted and furnished, and now offers the comforts of a home to all who may favor us with their patronage. The Table will at all times be well provided, and no pains will be spared to render the visit of our Guests agreeable.

Charges Always Reasonable.

STAGES are run by the Proprietor from **Woodbourne** to **Neversink** and **Grahamsville** and return, on Wednesday and Saturday; and to **Ellenville** and return, on Tuesday and Saturday of each week. Two Daily Stages also leave this House, one at 11:30 A. M., to connect with the Midland Railroad at Centerville; and one at 3 P. M., for Liberty.

A GOOD HALL,

Thirty by Fifty Feet, on the Ground Floor, for Public Entertainments.

Good Barns and Stabling Attached.

BUCKEYE Mower and Self-Raking Reaper, the most Perfect Harvester in the World. Adriance, Platt & Co., 165 Greenwich St., New York. See Card on Map.

ALL Orders by Mail promptly attended to at W. & G. STRONG'S Book Store, Monticello, Sullivan County, N. Y.

A notice in a local paper announced Woodbourne's first resort. "The Woodbourne Hotel is being fitted up for summer boarders. We understand that parties from the city have already engaged rooms at this place." A full-page advertisement in the business directory for Sullivan County announced its opening in 1872. Operated by John H. Waldorf, the hotel was located within the town. This advertisement boasted, "The Table will at all times be well provided." In the silver age, as in the golden age of Sullivan County, abundant food mattered.

The Todd Homestead grew from a farmhouse to a resort where guests enjoyed sitting on the capacious porch and eating substantial meals. Many, no doubt, went to the regular dances held nearby in the Woodbourne Casino, where they mingled with the guests from the other local boardinghouses and hotels.

The Knoll, built *c.* 1900 by Dr. J.A. Munson, was Woodbourne's showplace. The towered hotel, which stood on an elevation overlooking Neversink River, was locally famous for its flower gardens, which appeared on many postcards. The Knoll eventually became a rooming house called the Woodcrest Villa, which burned in December 1968.

Posing for a group picture was a popular part of summer. Traveling photographers went from place to place. Howard Wood of Hurleyville photographed guests at the Merritt House (above), operated by Silas Merritt, and August Guntlow's Mountain Spring House (below), both in Woodbourne, *c.* 1905. The Mountain Spring House's "depot wagon" is visible in the background. It was available to take guests to town, where they might shop at the Curio, a general-merchandise store operated by August Guntlow.

Hotel

Lawrence,

L. W. LAWRENCE,

PROPRIETOR.

Loch Sheldrake, Sullivan County, N. Y.

ACCOMMODATE 100. TWENTY MINUTES FROM R. R. STATION. HIGH GROUNDS OVERLOOKING THE LAKE. OWN LIVERY. LONG DISTANCE TELEPHONE. TWO MAILS DAILY. SPECIAL RATES JUNE AND SEPTEMBER.

NO BAR. NO CONSUMPTIVES OR HEBREWS.

Tarnishing the silver age was its blatant anti-Semitism. The Hotel Lawrence stated its policy firmly in an advertisement in *Summer Homes*: "NO BAR. NO CONSUMPTIVES OR HEBREWS." Changing ownership, it became the Overlook Hotel, which surprising really did overlook redundantly named Loch Sheldrake Lake. The Sha-Wan-Ga Lodge (below), near Wurtsboro, was the first major Christian-only hotel to become Jewish owned. Within a season, advertising changed from "Refined Christian House" to "Dietary Laws Observed." Eventually, the Overlook became Jewish, too, as the golden age began. Pleasure, not "refinement," became the hallmark of the new era.

Four

THE GOLDEN AGE

Fun and a hint of sex was key to the Borscht Belt, where innovative hotel owners were always working to extend the season from the traditional July–August period. The mixture of the religious and the secular was always strange: "Spend SHVUOTH AND DECORATION [Memorial] DAY with us."

Virtually all of the Borscht Belt hotel owners and their guests had either been born in eastern Europe or their parents or grandparents had. Popular image holds that all eastern European Jews arrived in steerage, dressed as peasants, and landed at Ellis Island. Many did. Others came over in a more fashionable mode. The author's maternal grandmother arrived cabin class on the *SS Bremen.* She always looked down on his paternal grandparents who did travel via steerage but who entered through Castle Garden, before Ellis Island was fully functional. The Jacobs

family—mother, father, and eight children (seven boys and one girl)—arrived looking stylish, if modest, on the Cunard Lines' *Aquitania* before World War I. Ben Jacobs (standing, fourth row, third from the right) and Julie Jacobs (standing, fifth row, sixth from the right) became partners with their wives in owning the Karmel Hotel in Loch Sheldrake. Their father, Sam Jacobs, stands in the fifth row, fourth from the right.

Julie Jacobs (left), Ben Jacobs (center), and cousin Perry Katz (right) were the owners and managers of the Karmel Hotel *c.* 1967. Author of *Catskill Culture*, Phil Brown, who worked at the Karmel as a waiter, remembers Julie Jacobs well. "He oversaw the kitchen . . . where he supervised meals . . . brandishing a giant serving spoon . . . and, when really angry, waved the spoon threateningly." In the early 1970s, the Karmel Hotel went bankrupt along with many other small and medium hotels that had flourished in the golden age.

Judy Jacobs (see page 2) and Franklin Kreutzer, engaged in the summer of 1962, pose in front of the handball court. Judy recalls, "To the left is the outdoor pool. To the right is the baseball field where . . . guests would play the Shady Nook Bungalow guests. This depended on whether or not the 'cesspool' under the baseball field was flooded that day." Today, the Karmel is a summer acting camp called Stage Door Manor. The complex is remarkably intact.

Judy Jacobs and Lester Katz, a bus boy at the Karmel Hotel, pose in front of the Junior Building in 1957. Lester "is the brother," Judy notes, "of Lawrence (Larry) Kasher who produced the Broadway show, 'Silk Stockings,' and also produced the movie 'Pete's Dragon.' He worked as a waiter." The future accomplishments of Catskill waiters and busboys, all college boys, is the stuff of legend.

In the 1920s, a craze for all things Spanish spread across America. "My Adobe Hacienda" was a hit song. Always trying to be on the cutting edge, Sullivan County resort owners adopted what came to be known as Sullivan County Mission with gusto. California missions seen in Zorro films became familiar. The facades of buildings like the Mission of San Diego del Alcala in California (above) became the model for many hotels. The Fulton House (see page 45) was extensively remodeled into the New Empire Hotel in the 1920s. The White Lake resort was photographed in the early 1970s as "the Empire declined."

The Flagler Hotel, the Borscht Belt's first grand hotel, got its Spanish face in the 1920s. Developed by Asias Fleisher and Philip Morgenstern, the hotel, pictured in the 1960s, was the first in the region to have in-room telephones. The Flagler, its main building demolished, is now the Crystal Run School, a facility for adults with developmental disabilities. When the hotel was at its prime, the author worked as a caddy at its pioneering golf course.

Many of the small-town synagogues that were built by Jewish farmers, businesspeople, and resort owners were also done in mission style. The Ulster Heights Synagogue still has services on the High Holidays. Like other surviving Sullivan County synagogues, it is now on the National Register of Historic Places.

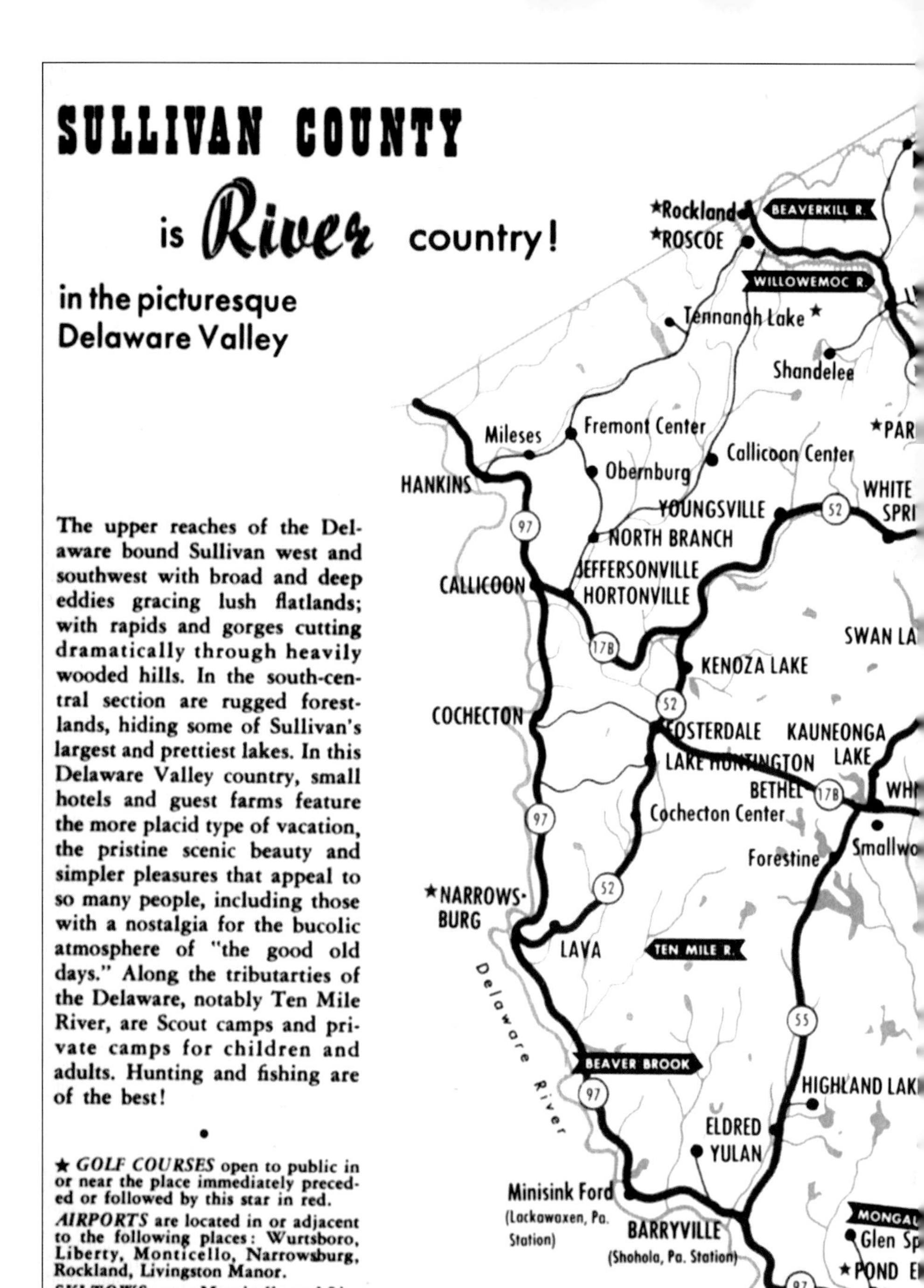
SULLIVAN COUNTY
is River country!
in the picturesque
Delaware Valley
The upper reaches of the Delaware bound Sullivan west and southwest with broad and deep eddies gracing lush flatlands; with rapids and gorges cutting dramatically through heavily wooded hills. In the south-central section are rugged forestlands, hiding some of Sullivan's largest and prettiest lakes. In this Delaware Valley country, small hotels and guest farms feature the more placid type of vacation, the pristine scenic beauty and simpler pleasures that appeal to so many people, including those with a nostalgia for the bucolic atmosphere of "the good old days." Along the tributarties of the Delaware, notably Ten Mile River, are Scout camps and private camps for children and adults. Hunting and fishing are of the best!
★ GOLF COURSES open to public in or near the place immediately preceded or followed by this star in red.
AIRPORTS are located in or adjacent to the following places: Wurtsboro, Liberty, Monticello, Narrowsburg, Rockland, Livingston Manor.
SKI TOWS: near Monticello and Livingston Manor; also on several hotel properties.
★Rockland
★ROSCOE
BEAVERKILL R.
WILLOWEMOC R.
Tennanah Lake ★
Shandelee
Mileses
Fremont Center
Callicoon Center
★PAR
HANKINS
Obernburg
YOUNGSVILLE
WHITE
SPRI
97
52
NORTH BRANCH
JEFFERSONVILLE
CALLICOON
HORTONVILLE
SWAN LA
17B
KENOZA LAKE
COCHECTON
OSTERDALE
KAUNEONGA
LAKE
BETHEL
Cochecton Center
Forestine
Smallwo
★NARROWS-
BURG
LAVA
TEN MILE R.
Delaware River
55
BEAVER BROOK
HIGHLAND LAK
ELDRED
YULAN
Minisink Ford
(Lackawaxen, Pa. Station)
BARRYVILLE
(Shohola, Pa. Station)
MONGAU
Glen Sp
★POND E

In the early 1950s, the Sullivan County Board of Supervisors published a booklet touting the county's virtues. The Ulster County resort towns such as Ellenville, Ulster Heights, and Kerhonkson are located to the right of the county line. Most of the Jewish resorts were located within an area bounded by Routes 52, 17, 178, and 209. This is the area today where many of

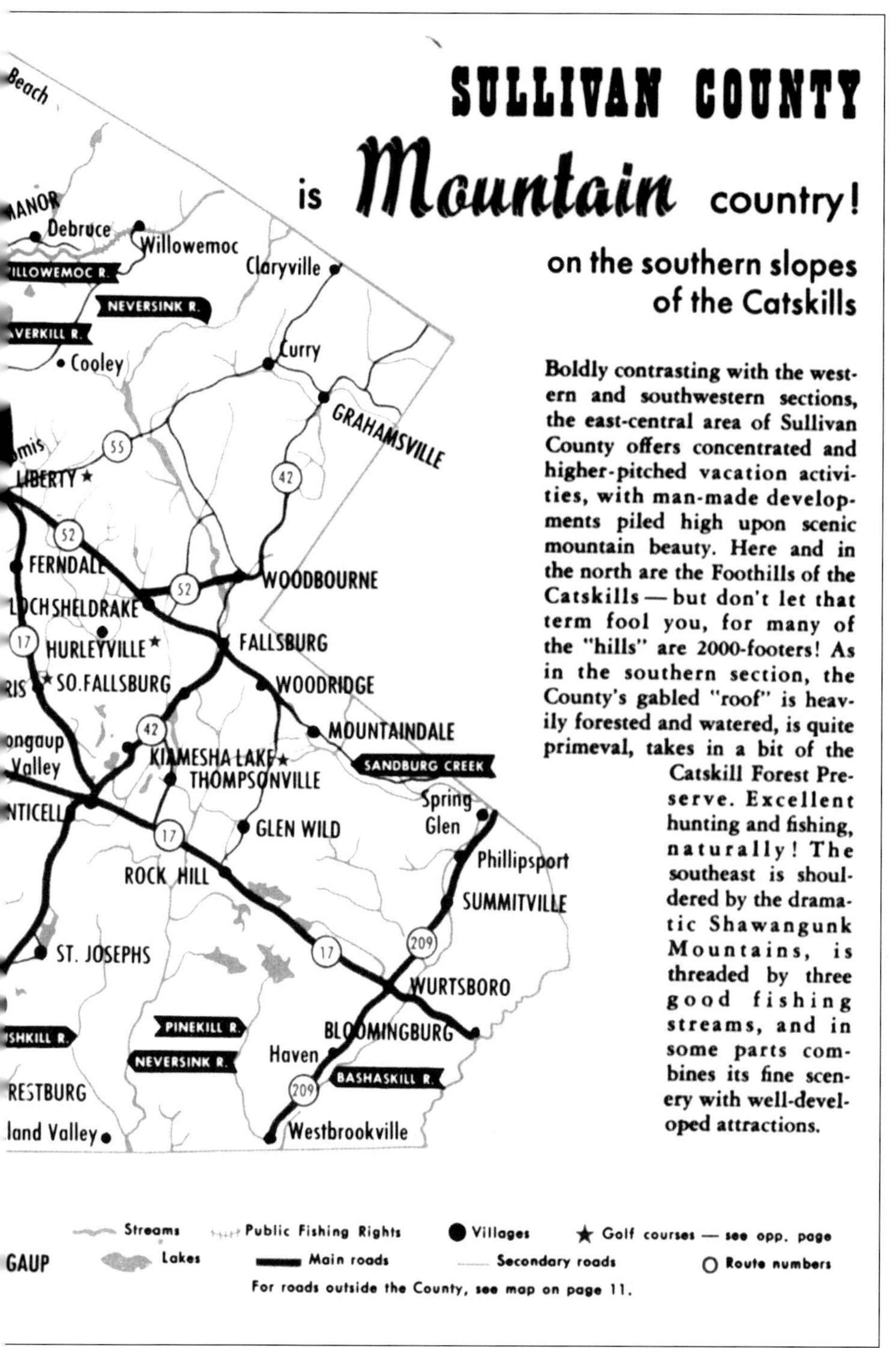

SULLIVAN COUNTY is *Mountain* country!

on the southern slopes of the Catskills

Boldly contrasting with the western and southwestern sections, the east-central area of Sullivan County offers concentrated and higher-pitched vacation activities, with man-made developments piled high upon scenic mountain beauty. Here and in the north are the Foothills of the Catskills — but don't let that term fool you, for many of the "hills" are 2000-footers! As in the southern section, the County's gabled "roof" is heavily forested and watered, is quite primeval, takes in a bit of the Catskill Forest Preserve. Excellent hunting and fishing, naturally! The southeast is shouldered by the dramatic Shawangunk Mountains, is threaded by three good fishing streams, and in some parts combines its fine scenery with well-developed attractions.

New York City's Hasidic and ultra-Orthodox summer. Today, many Jewish New Yorkers have summer homes in western Sullivan County along the Delaware River, which was mostly out of bounds to Jews during the golden age.

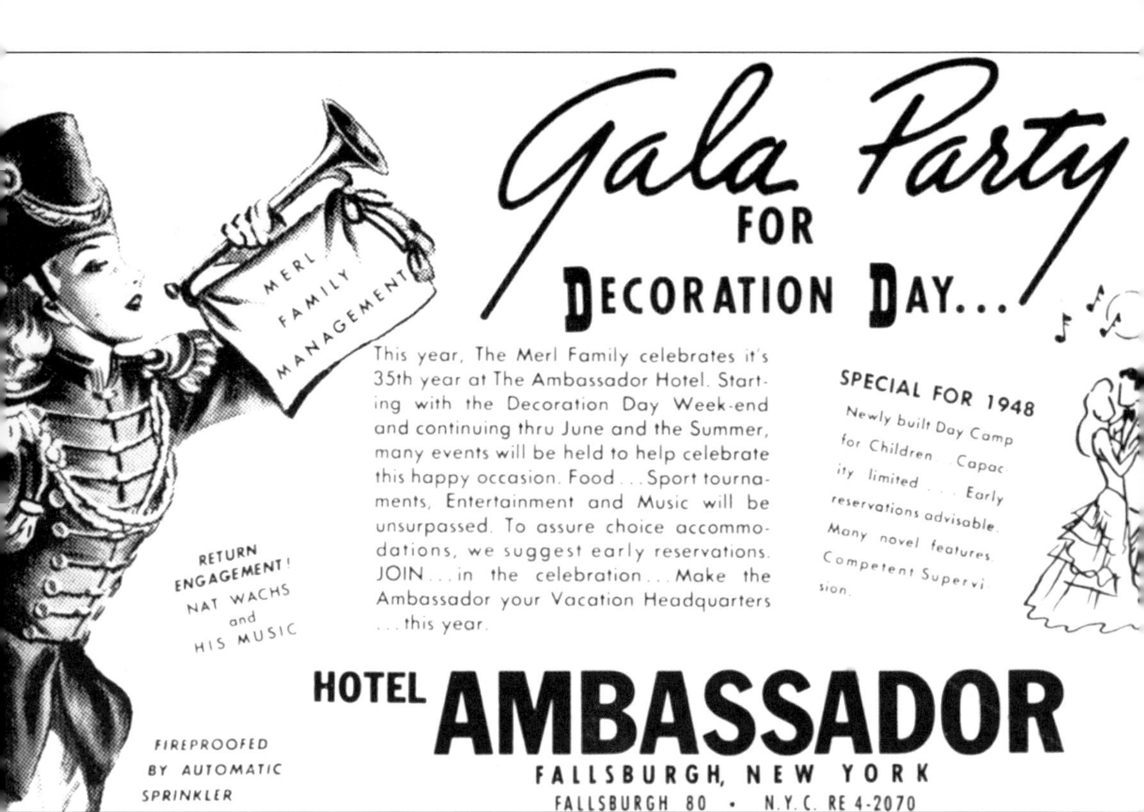

The Merl family, who owned the Ambassador Hotel in South Fallsburg, were in the fore—always offering their guests something new. In 1948, theirs was one of the first hotels to offer a day camp, where children could miraculously disappear so adults could play. Capacity was really "limited" to all guests. In the 1950s, the Ambassador sported the Catskills' first real nightclub, the Moulin Rouge.

- THRIFTY REDUCED AUGUST RATES -

AUGUST 10th TO LABOR DAY

MID-WEEK SPECIAL • 4 DAYS - 3 NIGHTS

FROM $32.50

Labor Day House Party Week-End

Three Full Days

$37.50 TO $55.00

Entertainment — Cocktail Party

Mid-Nite Supper

ROSH HASHONAH WEEK-END

September 12 - September 14

Two Full Days

$29.00 TO $44.00

CHILDREN: to age 11 .... 2/3 Rate

Religious Services on Premises

Entertainment — Cocktail Party

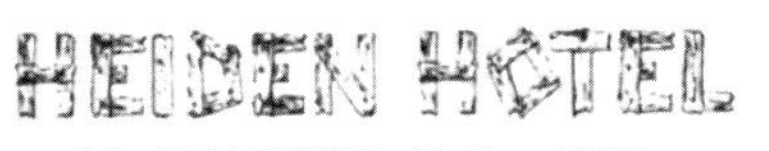

SO. FALLSBURG, N. Y. - 12779

For Reservations:
New York City Phone
244 - 5690

Late August was always slow at the hotels, which usually offered special rates, as in this 1950s flier. The flier also gives rates for special weekends—Labor Day and Rosh Hashana. It emphasizes the secular nature of most hotel guests; the Rosh Hashana heading "Religious Services on Premises" is in much smaller type than "Entertainment—Cocktail Party." Years after it closed, the Heiden Hotel was used as the setting for *Sweet Lorraine*, an exceptional movie about Catskill hotel life.

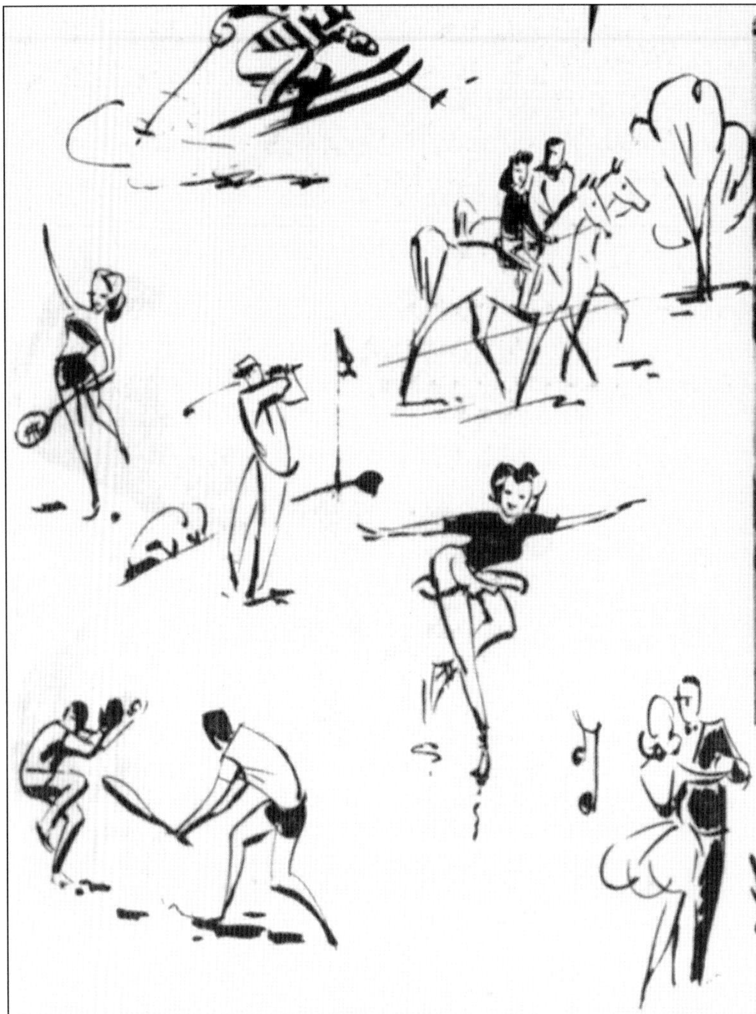

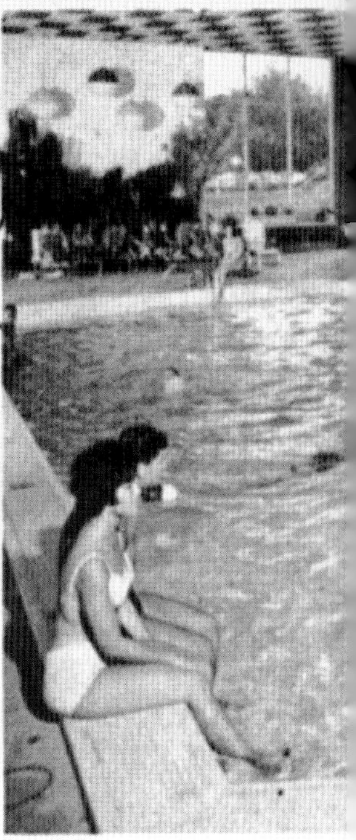

Ar

. . .
the
aro
birc
cha
mos
Hea
mas
'go

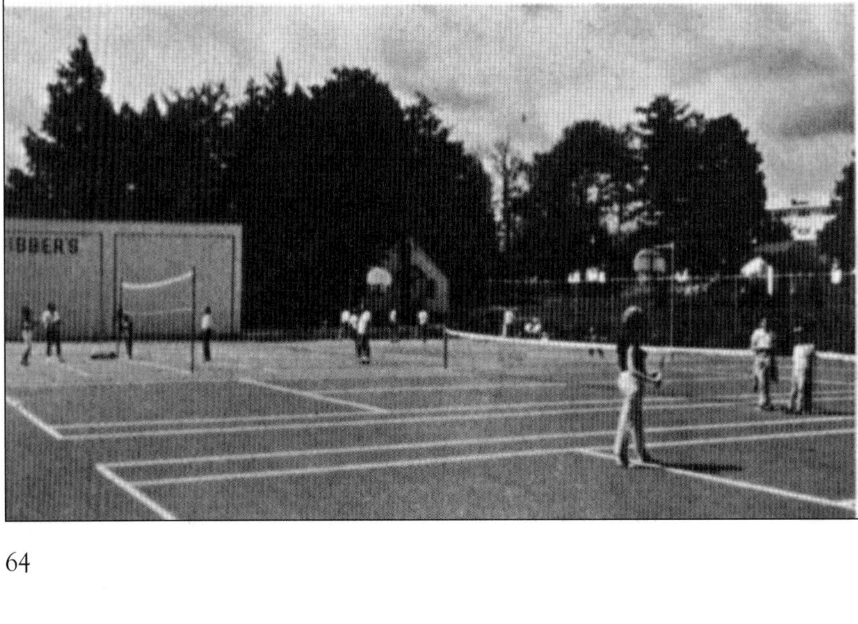

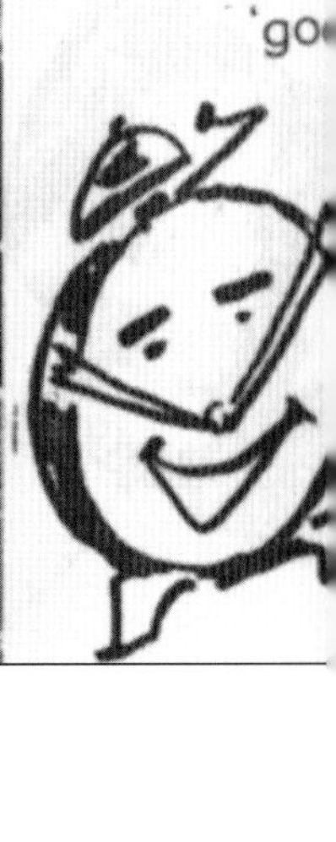

nd the Clock...
birds flock to the Hotel Gibber where
ways something exciting going on, right
e clock, right around the year. Water
head for the Rotunda Indoor Pool - a
circle of gleaming glass enclosing the
utiful indoor pool, anywhere. Complete
ub facilities adjoin the pool area, with
team rooms & exercise machine for that
over' feeling.

hotel
Gibber
KIAMESHA LAKE
NEW YORK
Tel.: (914) 794-6900

The Hotel Gibber was at its zenith in the 1960s. Its facilities and special features were those found at all major resorts. The "Around the Clock" brochure sounds like a modern cruise ship advertisement. Like many hotel owners, the proprietors also had a hotel in Miami Beach, the Cadet. After standing empty for a number of years, the Gibber was purchased in 1993 by the Hasidim of Yeshiva Viznitz in Williamsburg.

The owners and staff of the Maple Court Hotel pose in their kitchen in 1941. A small hotel with a very small, hardworking staff, it had a maximum capacity of 80 guests. Alice Gutter, a daughter of the owners, provides a key. "The staff in 1941: the milkman making a delivery; two busboys; Mama, chief cook and baker; Aunt Ethel, second cook; [Alice Gutter] the author,

bookkeeper, and salad-maker; J.N., my Dad, head waiter and everything else; my sister Vivian, governess and general helper; John, the year round handy man, trainable but not educable. Missing: Fanny, the chambermaid."

Large hotels had very large staffs. The dining room staff poses in 1956 at Kutsher's Country Club in Monticello. The young men were all college students who were chosen for their athletic talents and their ability to dance as well as for dining room skills. Staff played basketball in an organized hotel league to amuse guests. Others were expected to dance with female guests in the nightclub. Members of the Kutsher family stand in the back row. The

gentleman dressed in a tuxedo is Nat Symms, longtime maître d' at the hotel. The 1950s were still a formal time when male waiters were all expected to wear bow ties and jackets in the dining room. Kutsher's still operates today. If a similar picture were taken today, however, the waitstaff would represent a veritable United Nations of nationalities. Most would be professional waiters; few, if any, would be students.

Brown's Hotel Royal was probably about 40 years old when Sylvia and William Brown bought it in 1946 for $21,000, and they only owned it until 1952, when they lost it in a mortgage foreclosure. Reverting to the name Hotel Royal, it was sold in 1954 to Sol Pasternack, who owned it until 1991. The hotel's new owners, Scott Samuelson and Edward Dudek, spent two years transforming the run-down lakefront place into an upscale bed-and-breakfast called the Bradston, which features a popular cabaret as well.

At a small hotel like Brown's Hotel Royal, many of the guests were also relatives—or were they staff? It was never clear. A toddler cousin, clearly a guest, poses *c.* 1949 on the sliding board, or "sliding pon" in local parlance.

Cousin Gloria Klein is pictured at Brown's Hotel Royal in 1946. Notice that no one ever bothered to put the Brown name on the hotel. To the left, Klein poses next to a front-lawn flower bed. The canna, with its large leaves and bright colors, was almost the official flower of the Catskills. Every hotel had them.

In 1931, Philip and Mali Brown (seated, center) celebrated their 50th wedding anniversary at Leibowitz's Pine View Lodge in Fallsburg. Their son William, who later ran Brown's Hotel Royal, sits next to his parents. The Pine View was a very successful religious hotel that the

Leibowitz family bought in 1916. At its height, it could hold 450 guests and 50 to 70 children. It operated until 1982, when "the adjoining state prison [outside] Woodbourne took it by eminent domain to add a minimum security facility," according to the *Catskill Culture*.

Author Sidney Offit's 1959 novel about life in the Catskills is a *roman à clef* about the Aladdin Hotel in Woodbourne, which he calls the Hotel Sesame. Until his marriage into the Komito family in the 1950s, Offit had never been in the Catskills, but several summers working at the family hotel as kitchen steward and concession operator taught him the ins and outs of the business. His descriptions of kitchen life in a hotel have never been equaled.

In the 1930s, Carrie Komito's parents bought the Levbourne Hotel in Woodbourne, which Carrie and her husband ran for many years. They changed the resort's name to the Aladdin in the 1950s to modernize it at the same time as they converted the casino into a nightclub called the Ali Baba Room and added an indoor swimming pool. Carrie ran the hotel until 2000. She is seen checking a guest in when she was 92 (in 1993). The annex at the Aladdin is little changed from when it was originally built except for the new rooms added on the first-floor level.

The Route 17 Quickway remains the gateway for most visitors to Sullivan County. Built in the 1950s, it reduced the time of a trip to the mountains from New York City to two to three hours from the four to seven hours common before. At each exit, you were greeted with billboards,

large and small, mostly advertising hotels. Not one of the hotels advertised at exit 107 in the 1950s now operates. However, some of the buildings are now used as religious camps, ashrams, bungalow colonies, and apartment complexes.

There were so many hotels in Sullivan County that popular names like "Overlook" and "Lakeside" were used multiple times. The Lakeside Hotel in South Fallsburg sounded like a fun spot in 1935, when the sender of the postcard above wrote, "Having a swell time. Saw the pansy revue from the Wonder Bar last night. Swell band & nice fellows. They call me Babs. . . . Love, Blanche." The Lakeside Inn and Country Club in Ferndale advertised "spacious and airy rooms [that] have modern appointments for every comfort." In 1955, when operated by Charlie Berkowitz, the hotel burned. Liberty firefighter Dewey Borden remembered that the fire caused the building to "fold up like an accordion," narrowly missing a number of volunteer firemen.

MAIN BUILDING OF THE LAKESIDE INN AND COUNTRY CLUB, FERNDALE, NEW YORK

The Overlook Hotel and the Victoria Mansion dominated the Loch Sheldrake skyline *c.* 1915. The Overlook (above, left) was once the restricted Hotel Lawrence (see page 52). The Overlook in Ferndale (below) was a religious hotel that billed itself as "the House of Comfort," which offered "All Modern Improvements."

The West End Hotel in Loch Sheldrake was a small place that had been built in late 19th century in a mixture of styles, including the Second Empire. In this 1930s card, a lot of visual attention was given to the large front porch.

The Evans Hotel in Loch Sheldrake grew into a large enterprise, the place (according to an advertisement) to "live, laugh and enjoy the ultimate in vacation happiness." Early in the 20th century, however, it was an overgrown farmhouse sporting a fashionable mansard roof. Today, the hotel has evolved into Vacation Village, one of the region's most expensive Orthodox resort colonies, which combines new single-family vacation homes with the entertainment complex of the Evans in its prime.

The Grand Hotel features a typical large main house with cottages often called "bungalows." Note especially the imposing entry walk flanked by pillars. Today, stone pillars are often all that remain of many hotels. Author Phil Brown remembers that his mother cooked at the Grand for owner Maxie Schmidt, a nice person, an often rare quality in an owner as viewed by his or her employees. A guest, in 1946, writes, "Having a swell time and it's wonderful to send cards instead of receiving them."

Gluck's Hillside Hotel in Kiamesha was proud of its tennis courts and its swimming pool, complete with cabanas. The hotel owner apparently liked flowers. Hanging planters on the porch were not common at Catskill hotels.

Many hotels had a special emphasis or flavor. In its advertisements, the Pioneer Country Club offered "an adventure in luxury at modest rates." It was also one of the first ultra-Orthodox hotels in the mountains. Most of its dining room staff were yeshiva students. One modern Orthodox man recalls of the Pioneer, "To us, it was the orthodox Mountains, not just the Jewish Mountains."

Various labor unions and workman's rights organizations had Sullivan County hotels that were run for their members, where a vacation could be had for an even cheaper price than the modest hotels charged. One of the first of these was the Workingmans Circle in Liberty. This postcard was mailed in 1917. The clientele of the hotel was known for its leftist leanings.

The White Roe Hotel near Livingston Manor was a singles-only hotel that only took weekly guests—from Sunday to Sunday. Athletics were emphasized, but the White Roe was one of the few golden-age hotels not to have a pool. Guests swam in the lake. John Weiner, an owner, recalls not being happy unless he had booked two people into every bed. The White Roe offered a special premium: a free week to any couple who married after meeting at the hotel. So many couples met there that management had to cut the time offered down to a weekend.

The Commodore Hotel on Spruce Lake in South Fallsburg was very proud of its children's day camp, which was a new selling point. Parents could now vacation completely with the children returned after supper—just in time for the "night patrol," or roving babysitters, to take over while the parents dined and danced until 3:00 a.m. if they chose.

Tennis courts were a must for a hotel with any pretensions, although they were not as heavily used as they are at the few surviving resorts today. Charles and Lillian Brown's always tried to keep up. Brown's today is a condominium complex, and the tennis courts are still well maintained.

A men's beauty contest was always good for a laugh. This purely amateur drag show was held at the Granite Hotel in Kerhonkson in 1962. It is perhaps the illegitimate child of the quintessential Catskill entertainment: the mock marriage, in which a man played the bride and the woman played the groom.

Jews were notoriously slow to buy drinks at bars, but every resort had to have a bar to show how modern it was. Bars were rarely profit centers. The modern cocktail lounge was at the Nevele Country Club in Ellenville. Many Jewish women in the postwar years became very blond and had their noses "done."

Comedian Jerry Lewis's parents had worked for Charles and Lillian Brown, and young Jerry actually lived with the Browns for several years. When the Browns built a new nightclub at their resort, which they promoted as "a bit of California at your doorstep," they naturally called it the Jerry Lewis Theatre Club. Continuing the California theme, they named the showroom (below) the Brown Derby after the famed West Coast haunt of the stars. Jerry Lewis's image was used in many advertisements in which the comedian proclaimed, "Brown's is My Favorite Hotel." Lewis would show up at the resort on occasion.

The Slutsky family owned several Catskill hotels, including the Arrow Head Lodge and the Fallsview, but their jewel was the Nevele Country Club. Its landmark round tower was added in the 1950s. This aerial view shows the beautiful setting as well as the many athletic facilities, including *two* outdoor swimming pools and an ice rink. The Nevele still exists today as the Nevele Grande Hotel, but it is no longer run like the more traditional Catskill resorts and is no longer owned by the founding family.

In 1932, Marilyn Brown poses in front of Leibowitz's Pine View Lodge, all dressed up for the party to celebrate her grandparents' 50th anniversary (see pages 72 and 73). Note the large cars in the background, which were widely admired as signs of prosperity during the Great Depression and were parked in front of hotels whenever possible.

Marilyn Brown's half-brother Phil (at age 12) poses at the Evans Kiamesha in South Fallsburg, about 30 years later. Phil and his parents were "mountain rats" who worked in the Catskills. He began working in hotel dining rooms at age 13 and continued until he went to graduate school. Today a professor of sociology at Brown University, he is the author of *Catskill Culture: A Mountain Rat's Memories of the Great Jewish Resort Area.*

Shenk's Paramount Hotel in South Fallsburg was at its height in 1970, when it offered guests a wide range of facilities and services. The hotel bragged that it was "the Ultimate in Resort Living." A large abstract sculpture greeted you at the International Style face grafted onto the

old Catskill mission-style hotel. In 1970, the rates for the hotel's best accommodations, with a television and a private bath and shower, were $165 per week per person, double occupancy. Today, Schenk's is an Orthodox camp, and the sculpture looks especially forlorn.

The Chalows, who ran the Irvington Hotel, were proud of their "spacious air conditioned Dining Room," which was the latest in 1960s style. They wanted you to note the new pink, brown, and green vinyl tile floor, which was avant-garde. If you got hungry between meals—always likely—you could also eat at the "New Nosherei & Canteen."

The kitchens of all the resorts were large, commercial, and much less decorative than the dining rooms they served. They were also hot and buzzed with activity. This view of the Karmel Hotel's kitchen in Loch Sheldrake was typical. Note the large pots and the hanging utensils.

Sylvia Brown was a chef at a number of Catskill resorts, including her own short-lived Brown's Hotel Royal (see page 70). She was an excellent cook who was concerned about the appearance as well as the taste of her food. She cooked at small and medium hotels only; the large places would not hire a woman chef. For a number of years, she worked at Chait's in Accord. In the 1970s, she is seen in Chait's kitchen and setting up a luncheon buffet in the dining room.

Chaits

Menu

* *

LUNCH

Saturday, September 5, 1970

Chilled Sacramento Tomato Juice

Roman Chick Pea Soup
or
Chilled Borsht – Boiled Potato

Choice of:

Broiled Eastern Sea Bass Steaks – Cucumber Sauce

Hawaiian Luau (Sweet & Pungent Duck
(Chicken Livers & Chestnuts
(Polynesian Rice
(Fresh Pineapple Coconut

Garden Vegetable Plato with Stuffed Tomato

Fluffy Onion Omelette

Kashe Varnishkes — Buttered Spinach

Cold Entrees:

Tuna or Salmon Steak Salad Platter
Imported Sardine and Hardboiled Egg Salad, garni
Bowl of Sour Cream with Boysenberries, Bananas, Sliced Fresh Fruit or Cottage Cheese.

Desserts:

Russian Coffee Cake — Wild Cherry Jello
Chocolate Pudding — Tapioca Pudding
Rainbow Sherbet
Chocolate, Vanilla or Butter Pecan Ice Cream

Coffee — Sanka — Tea — Milk

2:30 p.m. – ARTS & CRAFTS with STEVE KLEINMAN

3:30 p.m. – FOLK & SQUARE DANCING with KARL FINGER

6:30 p.m. – COCKTAILS and HORS D'OEUVRES in the Lounge

9:30 p.m. – DON SHERMAN – Comedian

Chait's Hotel in Accord was a kosher-style rather than kosher establishment. A number of hotels changed course in the 1960s to keep up with the perceived "more American tastes" of their clientele. It is humorous that this 1970s menu offers chilled borscht with boiled potato, the signature Catskill dish, along with a "Hawaiian Luau featuring Sweet and Pungent Duck and Chicken Livers & [water] chestnuts." Mixing meat and dairy in one meal is a kosher no-no.

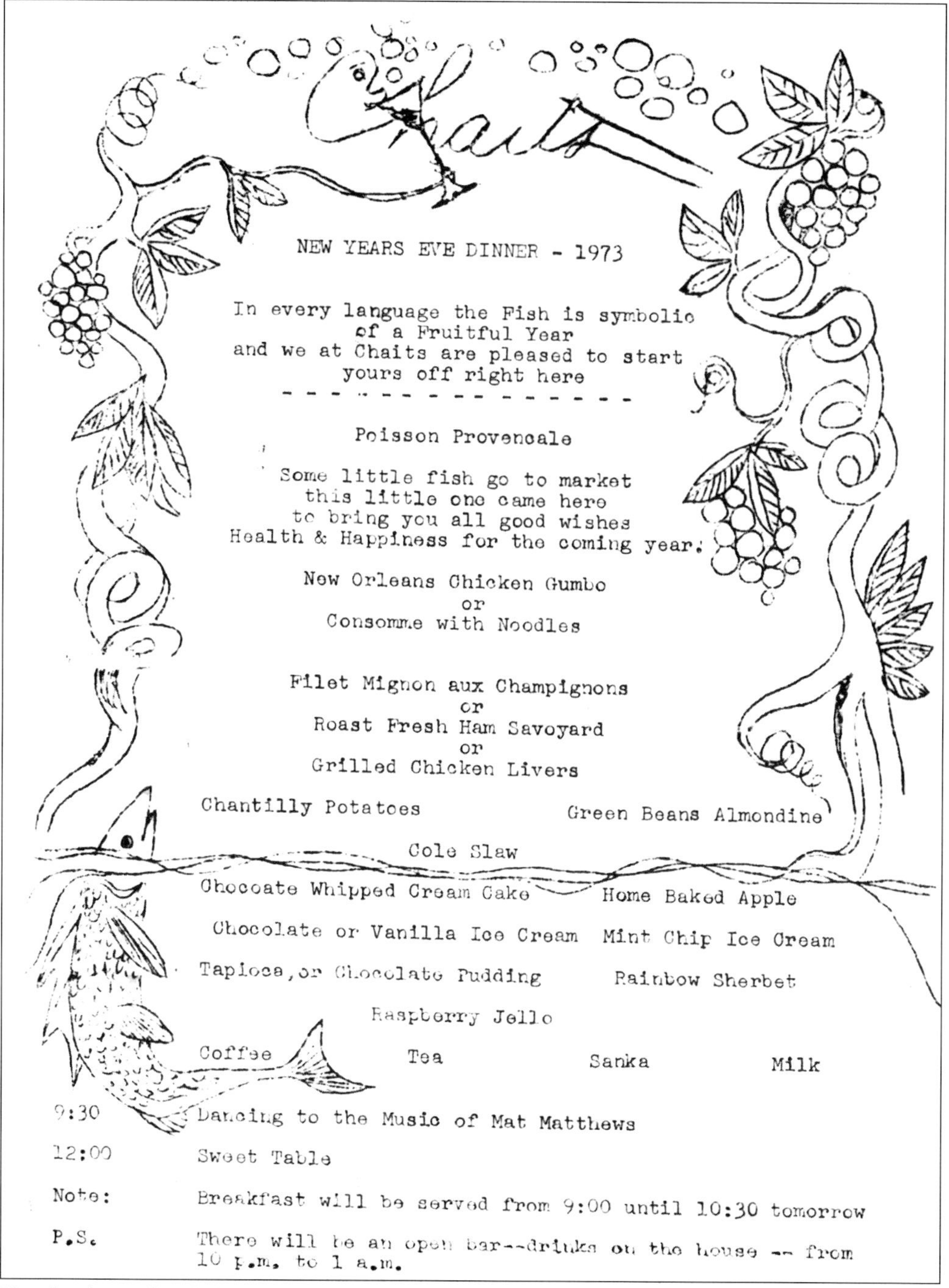

NEW YEARS EVE DINNER - 1973

In every language the Fish is symbolic
of a Fruitful Year
and we at Chaits are pleased to start
yours off right here

Poisson Provencale

Some little fish go to market
this little one came here
to bring you all good wishes
Health & Happiness for the coming year.

New Orleans Chicken Gumbo
or
Consomme with Noodles

Filet Mignon aux Champignons
or
Roast Fresh Ham Savoyard
or
Grilled Chicken Livers

Chantilly Potatoes   Green Beans Almondine

Cole Slaw

Chocoate Whipped Cream Cake   Home Baked Apple

Chocolate or Vanilla Ice Cream   Mint Chip Ice Cream

Tapioca, or Chocolate Pudding   Rainbow Sherbet

Raspberry Jello

Coffee   Tea   Sanka   Milk

9:30   Dancing to the Music of Mat Matthews

12:00   Sweet Table

Note: Breakfast will be served from 9:00 until 10:30 tomorrow

P.S.   There will be an open bar--drinks on the house -- from 10 p.m. to 1 a.m.

Hotels often offered elaborate New Year's Eve parties once they started to stay open in winter. Chait's was especially brave to offer roast ham, which was the ultimate rejection of tradition, but then Chait's was a hotel that catered to a left-leaning, liberated crowd.

Entertainment and entertainers came in all varieties in the Catskills. Two band members and their girlfriends pose in front of the Ulster Lake Hotel in 1948. They were 16 and 17 years old and earned $15 per week, plus room and board, for playing six nights a week and "cutting a show" on Saturday. The author's brother, Seymour Richman, is second from the right.

Probably the most popular performers in the Catskills were Myrna and Clare, the Barry Sisters, shown performing at Brickman's Hotel in South Fallsburg *c.* 1960. Beginning as the teenage Begelman Sisters, they toured the hotels. After they changed their stage name, they crossed over into the wider entertainment world, including an appearance on *The Ed Sullivan Show*. While they could perform beautifully in English, they are best known for their Yiddish repertoire, most of which has fortunately been preserved on their record albums (now available on compact disc).

Water has always been a popular draw in the Catskills. Every pond becomes a lake in advertisements. Here, at the Avon Lodge in Woodridge, guests row on "our own delightful Avon Lake where we [also] have . . . fishing or plain relaxing; skating in the winter too."

The earliest Catskill swimming pools were spring fed and often had earthen bottoms like this 1920s model on Schatzkamer's Farm, just north of Woodbourne. Its mailing address was Hurleyville, and its telephone number, in 1942, was Hurleyville 9R. Len Shenkin is in his sailor suit on a summer day.

The old unfiltered pools were places without many rules, where kids and adults could cavort in an atmosphere reminiscent of the "old swimming hole" of legend. In 1947, Len Shenkin balances on the shoulders of his father, Abe. It is a picture of pure joy. Cousin Larry Chenkin paddles while wearing a swimming vest. The site is Schatzkamer's Farm near Woodbourne.

Leibowitz's Pine View Hotel (formerly Pine View Inn) in Fallsburg was a large modern Orthodox resort in the 1960s. Liberal, it allowed mixed-sex swimming. Often, as here, pools were part of a sports complex. Shuffleboard and basketball courts are in the foreground.

The large sterile concrete tanks that were necessary at all resorts were seldom used by swimmers; rather, they were the center of sunbathing, poolside card games, and cha-cha lessons. The Fallsview in Ellenville was proud of its "mammoth filtered swimming pool and Rivera Patio Bar." The Fallsview still operates as a kosher hotel and is affiliated with the Nevele Grande.

The Harmony Country Club, on Lake Anawana near Monticello, called itself "the Big Hotel with the Homelike Atmosphere." In the background is the hotel's solarium, which housed a bar, restrooms, and storage space for the lounge chairs guests enjoyed.

The Stevensville Country Club at Swan Lake catered to a young crowd. It was a place where you would expect high divers to fly through the air. Given that only two figures, carefully posed, are looking up, this is probably a trick shot.

Indoor swimming pools were a must. One hotel owner ruefully said, "When people call up, they ask if we have an indoor pool. If we don't, they hang up. Even if they never swim." The New Hotel Gibber in Kiamesha had an artist's version of their new pool, probably done before the real one was installed. Note the palm trees—always a popular pool motif. The Concord, also in Kiamesha, had elaborate mural decoration. From an adjoining bar, viewers could look into the pool, below the surface.

Indoor pools followed one of the two basic patterns—they either emphasized a relationship to the outdoors, or they hid it. At the Stevensville in Swan Lake (above), the pool was isolated from its surroundings. At the Hotel Brickman in South Fallsburg, it opened on to the landscape. Indoor pools were generally the only place where food and drink was unavailable.

The Tamarack Lodge in Greenfield Park offered a wide range of sports. While boating, fishing, and archery were generally included in a guest's daily fee, horseback riding was not. Only the largest hotels could maintain their own stables. Smaller places would often ferry equestrian-minded guests to an off-site stable. Similarly, guests would pay extra for some individual sports and dance lessons.

Handball, from the earliest days, was probably the most popular Borscht Belt sport. Many New York kids played the game using any vacant wall. Public parks also had handball courts. Come summertime and vacations, lots of men took to the courts. Women seldom played the game. Courts were often visible from the road and could do double duty as a billboard.

Romance was, of course, always a part of the Borscht Belt tradition. Young Jews marrying young Jews was viewed as essential, and in the heyday of the resort age, intermarriage was rare. To help you along, many hotels, including the Tamarack, had "flirtation walks" or "kissing arches." They were romantic—and cheap to build.

PANORAMA — The ultimate in accommodations — for those who demand the best.
NEW LOBBY — Unsurpassed in elegance and charm

The Sha-Wan-Ga Lodge in High View was the first large Sullivan County hotel to be sold to Jews (see page 52). By the 1960s, it had been developed into an exciting, modern resort that always had something of a racy reputation, but in truth, much of its gamy repute was earned in the 1930s and 1940s. By the 1960s, the hotel was catering to a family crowd. The senders of this postcard, Ros and Norm, write, "We're really having a wonderful time here. This hotel is lovely. The kids having a ball entering tournaments, etc. Swimming every day."

Grossinger's, along with the Flagler, pioneered winter sports in Sullivan County. Grossinger's toboggan run was a first. It joined cross-country and downhill skiing and outdoor and then indoor ice-skating in attracting guests. Winter, however (except for holidays and, later, for conventions), was always slow. When Grossinger's was founded near the turn of the century, it was located in Liberty Falls. Because *Liberty* and *tuberculosis* became synonymous, the town changed its name to Ferndale. Years later, Grossinger's would be the only Sullivan County hotel to have its own post office.

Lucille and Tony

present

"THE DANCE EVENT of THE YEAR"

at GROSSINGER'S

"THE RESORT CAPITAL OF THE WORLD"

Another Fabulous Weekend of Superlative Dance Demonstrations and Spectacles at the Famous Lucille and Tony 'University of the Dance' with a Faculty of the Outstanding Dance Masters in America Teaching and Demonstrating . . Hours and Hours of Free Instruction Spotlighting All the Major Dances of the Day and Previewing All the New Dance Trends.

Great Bands (accent on the Latin Bugaloo) . . . SIX Sumptuous Meals . . . Top Professional Dance Acts Stars in TWO Star-Studded Broadway Night Club Revues . . . THREE Days and TWO Nights of All the Fabulous Funtime Facilities and Excitements that Make Grossinger's the Nation's Most Glamourous Resort Playground . . .

If You Love Dancing, You Can't Afford to Miss this Memorable, Dancingest Weekend of the Year!

For Further Dance Information
Please write or call:
Lucille and Tony
Penthouse Dance Studio
101 West 57th Street
New York, N. Y. 10019
(212) PL 7-0418

Dance-In We

Friday to Sunday, Sept. 5

at

plus
A GALA
THE DANSANT
COCKTAIL
PARTY
and
ALL THE STORIED
AND FUN FACILIT
NEW YORK'S FA
RESORT HOT

Lucille and Tony
DANCE FESTI
will bring you
AN UNPARALLELED WEEKEND O
DEMONSTRATIONS AND FREE CLAS
(FOR FESTIVAL GUESTS ONLY) IN
PATTERNS.
presented by
FAMOUS DANCE INSTRU
plus

★ EXCITING PROFESSION "DANCIBITION" STAGE SH
★ GROSSINGER'S ACCUST BROADWAY ENTERTAINME
★ DANCING . . . MORNING, NO NIGHT . . . TO OUR OWN BAND A FAMOUS GUEST ORCHES

Dancing was a very popular Catskill activity. Most hotels would have poolside dancing during the day and, of course, nighttime dancing in the casino or nightclub. Many hotels, even modest ones, would have resident dance instructors to help keep the guests happy. The role of dance instructors is the theme of the presumed Catskill movie *Dirty Dancing*. Grossinger's even offered dance weekends. Its resident dance team, Lucille and Tony, were known beyond the Catskills and even maintained a New York studio. The top rate for a two-night stay in September 1963 was $80 per person, double occupancy. Rates started at $21 per day.

SHABAT SHALOM

Grossinger's took the Sabbath seriously, although there was often tension between the more religious ways of the Orthodox founders, Selig and Malka Grossinger, and their more liberal offspring, especially their daughter Jennie. The inside cover of this 1964 menu has a description of the Sabbath: "Eighteen minutes before sundown on Friday the Sabbath is ushered into the home by the kindling of the Sabbath light. Tradition has assigned this beautiful ceremony to the mother, because her mission is to kindle the light of the Torah in the hearts of her children."

Please refrain from smoking in the Lobbies or Dining Room on the Sabbath

The Sabbath Starts at 4:15 P.M.

APPETIZER

Chilled Spanish Melon
Cooled California Tomato Juice
Frosted Val Sweet Grape Juice

RELISH

Hearts of Crisp Lettuce en Branche
Spanish Queen Olives
Carrot Sticks
California Ripe Olives
Rosebud Radishes
Homemade Dill Pickles

ENTREE

Stuffed Freshwater Fish, Beet Horseradish

SOUP

Consomme Matzo Ball
Bouillon w Carolina Rice
Clear Broth en Tasse

DINNER

Roast Stuffed Lakewood Spring Chicken, Pan Gravy
Potted Brisket of Beef, Barley and Beans
Rolled Stuffed Cabbage, Hongroise
Roast Breast of Veal, Glaced Pineapple
Barbecued Ribs of Beef, Hot Mustard
Broiled Filet of Boston Bluefish, Fermiere
Boiled Young Fowl en Pot, Matzo Ball
Garden Vegetabde Dinner w Oven Baked Potato
Potato Pudding
Carrot Tzimmes

SALAD

Cole Slaw, Mexicana
Bowl of Fresh Fruit

Sabbath dinner was very traditional at Grossinger's, but it is amusing to note under the entree heading that gefilte fish has been Americanized into "Stuffed Freshwater Fish." Because of the Sabbath, guests were asked not to smoke in public areas, but by the 1960s, there would be a show and dancing in the playhouse on Friday nights. To allow this, a fiction was created in which the hotel was "sold" to a Christian each Friday and "repurchased" each Saturday at sundown.

Grossinger's was especially proud of its Passover Seders, which featured star cantors, such as Richard Tucker or Robert Merrill, and large choirs. It was very popular for families to spend Passover in a resort so that the mother of an observant family did not have to go through the arduous task of making the house kosher for Passover, which included not only a ritual cleaning

but changing all of the pots, cutlery, and dishes. Hotels always ordered new dishes for Passover and used them for the rest of the year, but their kitchens, too, had to be rigorously cleaned. The closer you sat to the choir, the more expensive were your accommodations. At smaller hotels, the rituals and the meals were simpler.

KUTSHER'S COUNTRY CLUB

News Letter

SPRING-SUMMER 2002 • MONTICELLO, NEW YORK • Tel: 800-431-1273 • www.kutshers.com

We're Always Here For You

For four generations our family has offered your family the perfect escape from the stress and strain of everyday life. So, there's probably never been a better time to experience the pleasures of Kutsher's than right now. Just let go and let Kutsher's do what we do best...to give you the most complete vacation possible.

You'll be relaxed and renewed in beautiful surroundings with fabulous entertainment, delicious food and every conceivable sports facility, including one of the best golf courses in the Northeast. And, possibly best of all, no airports and no hassles getting here and back home. We're still just an easy ninety minutes by car from New York City.

By now, we're sure you have heard that Park Place Entertainment, the world's largest gaming organization, is moving ahead on plans to build a magnificent casino hotel on a site just down the road from our current location. And they want to keep Kutsher's Country club operating in the same way it's been all these years with the Kutshers family at the helm. They are enthusiastic about their progress and so are we. We believe in the success of this enterprise, bringing with it wonderful opportunities not just for Kutsher's but for the entire Catskill region as well.

In the meantime, remember when you want to get away from it all, Kutsher's will always be here for you: The best short distance destination for safe, hassle-free, fun-filled and totally carefree vacationing pleasure.

Mark Kutsher

There are only two golden age resorts left that are owned and operated by a founding family—the Raleigh (owned by the Ratners) and Kutsher's (now in its fourth generation)—but their days are, perhaps, numbered. This 2002 newsletter explains that there are plans for Kutsher's if gambling comes to Sullivan County.

DRINK SUGGESTIONS
SEA BREEZE OR SCREW DRIVER $2.50

GOOD EVENING DINNER

FRUIT OR JUICE: CHILLED MELON IN SEASON
OR
CHOICE OF YOUR FAVORITE JUICE

RELISH: ASSORTED RELISH TRAY
TOSSED GARDEN GREENS, RUSSIAN DRESSING

FISH: *STUFFED FRESH WATER FISH, BEET HORSERADISH
*JELLIED NORTHERN YELLOWPIKE, HOMESTYLE

SOUP: *CONSOMME WITH FLUFFY MATZO BALL
*POTAGE ALA REINE
*CLEAR BROTH, EN TASSE

ENTREE:
BRAISED FRESH BRISKET OF BEEF, BEAN & BARLEY CHOLENT
ROAST STUFFED HALF MARYLAND SPRING CHICKEN
ITALIAN STYLE SPAGHETTI WITH MEATBALLS
ROAST ROULADE OF TENDER YOUNG VEAL, PINEAPPLE SLICE
ITALIAN STYLE CHICKEN CACCIATORE, PASTA
ROLLED STUFFED CABBAGE LEAVES HONGROISE
POTTED CHOPPED CLUB STEAK WITH SAUTEED ONIONS
*BOILED BEEF FLANKEN WITH BOUILLION VEGETABLES
*SAUTEED FILET OF MASSACHUSETTS BAY HADDOCK, PARSLEY GARNE
*STEAMED SELECTED PLYMOUTH ROCK PULLET, BOILED POTATO
*BOUQUETIERE OF GARDEN VEGETABLES, STEAMED POTATO

NOODLE PUDDING CARROT & PRUNE TZIMMES
* THESE ITEMS ALSO AVAILABLE FOR SALT RESTRICTED DIETS, PLEASE SPECIFY *

DESSERT:
APPLE STRUDEL FRUIT FLAVORED SHERBET
CHOCOLATE SEVEN LAYER CAKE GOLDEN SPONGE CAKE
COCONUT MACAROONS DINNER COOKIES
CLOVER HONEY CAKE RASPBERRY GEL
DIET APPLE STRUDEL

BEVERAGES: BREWED DECAFFEINATED COFFEE
ORANGE PEKOE TEA CAFE NOIR
PAREVE MARGARINE PAREVE MOCHA MIX

BRUCE AYMES, MAITRE D'
FRIDAY, AUGUST 25, 2000

K U T S H E R ' S C O U N T R Y C L U B

At Kutsher's, the meals served today are virtually identical to those served in the golden age. To eat in the dining room is a gastronomic lesson in historic preservation. The food is plentiful. Astute waiters often bring extra dishes of unordered food "for the table." Compare this Friday evening menu with that at Grossinger's in 1964 (see page 111). Long live gefilte fish and matzoh ball soup, no matter what they call them!

2002 SUMMER RATES

JUNE 30 - AUGUST 30, 2002

RATES PER PERSON-DOUBLE OCCUPANCY (ALL ROOMS WITH AIR CONDITIONING, REMOTE COLOR TV)

		MIDWEEK VACATIONETTE		
	7 Nights WEEKLY	6-Day, 5-Nite	5-Day, 4-Nite	4-Day, 3 Nite
MARQUIS				
Elevator, Climate Control, Refrigerator, Bath & Shower	$889	$575	$484	$369
TOWER SECTION				
Tower Special	$889	$575	$484	$369
Tower	$833	$560	$456	$348
600 SECTION				
Elevator	$777	$520	$428	$327
RIP VAN WINKLE				
Delux Rooms with Patio	$777	$520	$428	$327
Elevator, Deluxe Rooms	$742	$495	$412	$321
WINGS & POPLARS	$672	$440	$364	$279
3rd or 4th Adult in Room	$567	$405	$332	$255
CHILDREN'S RATES (In room with two adults)				
To Age 10 in Junior Dining Room	$287	$195	$156	$120
To Age 16 in Main Dining Room	$371	$260	$220	$171

10% OFF ALL SUMMER

on 3,4 and 5 Night Midweek Packages *(If reserved by June 17th)*

Kutsher's summer rates reflect the times. They are, of course, much higher than in the 1960s or 1970s, but they are significantly lower than the rates of the more elite Lake Mohonk (see page 36). In today's travel world, it is almost a bargain to vacation at Kutsher's.

Bestselling author Terry Kay (right) joins the author and his wife, Dr. M. Susan Richman, at a Saturday night dinner at Kutsher's in 2000. Dress is much more casual than it used to be. Kay's novel *Shadow Song* is set in Pine Hill, Ulster County, and is based on the summers he spent working at a Catskill resort that catered to German Jews in the 1950s. A Christian from Georgia, he brings fresh insights to a familiar story. The photograph was taken by a hotel photographer and sold to guests—a very old tradition.

Five
THE CATSKILLS AND FLORIDA

In the 1950s, the Levinson family, the owners of the Tamarack Lodge in Greenfield Park, were turning to a modernism being popularized in Florida. Today, we have cybercafes, but at that time, modern meant a "Televue Terrace."

Welcome

Tamarack is always ready with the makings of a sparkling vacation. Here you'll find 400 acres of fun facilities. For unexcelled comfort, you will enjoy the sunny, spacious rooms in the Main Lodge, Cabins, and the adjacent buildings. Most rooms have private or semi-private showers. During the day you'll thrill in the participation of sports on Tamarack's championship fields. After the sun goes down, the lights go up and activities center around Tamarack's playtorium. On stage you'll see your favorite stars of stage, screen, radio and television. After show time there's always dancing to two name bands. For a snack or a drink, meet in the air conditioned Sportsman's Lounge or Televue Terrace, where hilarity and good fellowship reigns supreme.

Produced in Magicolor by
Nat Steingart Assoc., So. Fallsburg, N. Y.

Main Building—Having a wonderful time!

Before the mid-1950s, Tamarack Lodge advertisements emphasized the establishment's traditional architecture but also its "air conditioned sportsman's Lounge or Televue Terrace, where hilarity and good fellowship reigns supreme." When the owners built a new hotel, the Algiers, in Miami Beach, they took an entirely different tack, as Modernism triumphed.

The 225-room Algiers Hotel, the address for which was "Oceanfront, 25th to 26th Street, Miami Beach," was a self-proclaimed "world-in-itself." It was built in 1951 by Dave Levinson, who had grown up as the son of a Jewish farmer in Greenfield Park, New York. The architect, Morris Lapidus (1902–2001), designed the most elaborate hotels Florida ever saw. At various times, Dave Levinson also owned or operated the Marlin, the Sorrento, and the Edge Water, but he always returned to Greenfield Park and the Tamarack Hotel.

The Laurels Country Club, on Sackett Lake near Monticello, was owned by the Novak family whose son Ben would change the face of Miami Beach, Florida. The Laurels was a successful hotel that offered its guests every service they could expect in a Catskill resort, including an 18-hole private golf course and clubhouse.

Modernism (as well as French nomenclature) was the preferred style for 1950s construction at the Laurels. The hotel's best rooms were to be found in the "New Deluxe Pierre—elegantly furnished, featuring Junior Suites—television, air conditioned." The poolside sports complex also reflected the new aesthetic, especially in the dramatic cabana. The buildings in the background are leftovers from an earlier era. Typically, the exteriors of subsidiary buildings were seldom altered, and most hotels were an architectural mishmash.

The symbolic summit of Miami Beach was reached when Ben Novak built the Fontainebleau Hotel in Miami Beach, which many Jews called "the southern Borscht Belt" and was widely joked about as being a suburb of New York City. Novak, who was born in the Bronx, grew up in the hotel business in Sullivan County. He wanted to build "the world's most pretentious hotel," and he did. The layout of the formal grounds, however, is reminiscent of the lawn in front of the Laurels Country Club on Sackett Lake (see page 120). Completed in 1954, the 14-story hotel was built on the former Harvey Firestone estate. One observer considered it to be "the most colossal . . . outrageous and controversial Miami Beach resort . . . hotel."

The architect of the Fontainebleau Hotel (named for a French royal palace) was Brooklyn-born designer Morris Lapidus (1902–2001), who was thoroughly grounded in Modernism but believed that architecture was a "broad form of merchandising." Rejecting the Modernist dictum "More is Less," he seems to have adopted the motto "Too much of a good thing is never enough." The Fontainebleau's ballroom held 5,000 and was famed for its floor shows featuring Hollywood stars. Buried out of sight was a *mikveh*, a ritual bath many Jewish resorts had. The lobby was spectacular with its Neoclassic overtones and its "stairway to nowhere" that was installed so that guests could make a grand entrance.

Russian-born Arthur Winarick wanted to create the grandest hotel in Sullivan County, and he did. Seeing the popularity of the Fontainebleau Hotel in Miami Beach, Winarick seized the opportunity to leave his chief competitor, Grossinger's, in a homey dust. He commissioned Fontainebleau architect Morris Lapidus to expand and remodel the Concord. In many ways, the resort became the "Fontainebleau North," right down to formal gardens. Where the Fontainebleau had only 14 acres, the Concord had 1,600. The Fontainebleau had the Atlantic; the Concord had Lake Kiamesha. Most Borscht Belt hotels attempted to emulate the Concord in the 1950s and 1960s. Many went bankrupt trying. The Concord, itself, went into a slow decline in the 1980s and closed in bankruptcy in the 1990s.

A guest visiting the Concord Hotel in 1968 wrote to friends, "This place is so big you really could get lost. . . . They handle 5000 people at one time." Another wrote, "This place is immense. . . . The dining room seats 3000. Bedrooms are large and comfortable." The hotel's nightclub, the Imperial Room, presented the same Hollywood entertainment that the Fontainebleau offered, and architect Morris Lapidus gave the Concord a "staircase to nowhere" as he had done at the Fontainebleau (see page 123) so guests could make their grand entrances. Out of sight was a jewelry kiosk where costume jewelry was sold during the week—and real jewelry during the weekend. A form of theatre was watching the ostentatious pay for expensive jewelry by peeling $100 bills from their large rolls. Those were more innocent and safer times.

Arthur Winarick and his general manager, Ray Parker (his son-in-law), positioned the Concord as the Borscht Belt's premier "all-year, all sports resort." Unlike Grossinger's and many other resorts, the Concord never branched out into Florida, although in architecture, it was the most Floridian place in the mountains. In the background of the vast artificially frozen ice rink, you can see pieces of the old Concord and a corner of a Lapidus-designed building. The Concord also had an indoor swimming pool and indoor tennis courts to make winter more bearable. An indoor ice rink let you skate in summer.

Every good Catskill or Florida vacation had to combine important elements—fun and perhaps a little naughty behavior. For the owners of resorts, the aim was, at whatever price range, to extract the maximum amount of money for their very perishable service. As noted in *To the Golden Cities*, it was a business designed "to convince a sucker spending $50 that he's actually spending $100." The postcard above was purchased by the author's parents when they honeymooned in the Catskills in 1931. It suggests the naughty. The 1930s card below sums up a great vacation for all sides: "I'M WEAK AND I'M DIZZY AND I HAVEN'T A DIME—BUT BOY! MY VACATION WAS A WHALE OF A TIME!" And the story goes on.

BIBLIOGRAPHY

Adams, Joey, and Henry Tobias. *The Borscht Belt.* New York: The Bobbs-Merrill Company, 1959.

Blumberg, Esterita. *Remember the Catskills: Tales by a Recovering Hotelkeeper.* Fleishmanns, New York: Purple Mountain Press, 1996.

Brown, Phil. *Catskill Culture: A Mountain Rat's Memories of the Great Jewish Resort Area.* Philadelphia: Temple University Press, 1999.

———, ed. *In the Catskills: A Century of the Jewish Experience in "The Mountains."* New York: Columbia University Press, 2002.

Conway, John. *Retrospect: An Anecdotal History of Sullivan County, New York.* Fleishmanns, New York: Purple Mountain Press, 1996.

Evers, Alf. *The Catskills: From Wilderness to Woodstock.* Garden City, New York: Doubleday and Company, 1972.

———, Elizabeth Cromley, Betsy Blackmar, and Neil Harris, eds. *Resorts of the Catskills.* New York: Architectural League of New York–St. Martins Press, 1979.

Frommer, Myrna Katz, and Harvey Frommer. *It Happened in the Catskills: An Oral History.* New York: Harcourt Brace Jovanovich, 1991.

Gold, David M., ed. *The River and the Mountains: Readings in Sullivan County History.* South Fallsburg, New York: Marielle Press, 1994.

Grossinger, Tania. *Growing Up at Grossinger's.* New York: David McKay, 1975.

Jacobs, Harvey. *Summer on a Mountain of Spice.* New York: Harper and Row, 1975.

Kanfer, Stefan. *A Summer World: The Attempt to Build a Jewish Eden in the Catskills.* New York: Farrar Straus Giroux, 1989.

Kay, Terry. *Shadow Song.* New York: Pocket Books, 1994.

Moore, Deborah Dash. *To the Golden Cities: Pursuing the American Dream in Miami and L.A.* New York: Free Press, 1994.

Offit, Sidney. *He Had It Made.* New York: Crown Publishers, 1959.

Pollack, Eileen. *Paradise, New York.* Philadelphia: Temple University Press, 1998.

Richman, Irwin. *The Catskills in Vintage Postcards.* Charleston, South Carolina: Arcadia Publishing, 1999.

———. *Sullivan County Borscht Belt.* Charleston, South Carolina: Arcadia Publishing, 2001.

Van Zandt, Roland. *The Catskill Mountain House.* New Brunswick, New Jersey: Rutgers University Press, 1966.

Wakefield, Manville B. *To the Mountains by Rail.* Grahamsville, New York: Wakefair Press, 1979.

Wallenrod, Reuben. *Dusk in the Catskills.* New York: Reconstructionist Press, 1957.